Not Just Another

Pretty Face

Not Just Another

Pretty Face

Edited by Louis Flint Ceci

Photographs by Dot

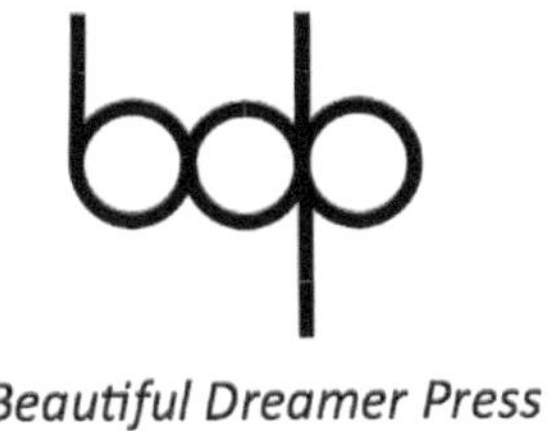

Beautiful Dreamer Press

Beautiful Dreamer Press
309 Cross St.
Nevada City, CA 95959
U.S.A.
www.BeautifulDreamerPress.com

Black and White Paperback Edition
Printed in the United States of America

ISBN: 978-0-9708310-6-4 (paperback)

Library of Congress Control Number: 2015919052

Front and back cover design by Tom Schmidt
Front and back photographs by Dot

For Bill Brent,

"Because it's fun."

CONTENTS

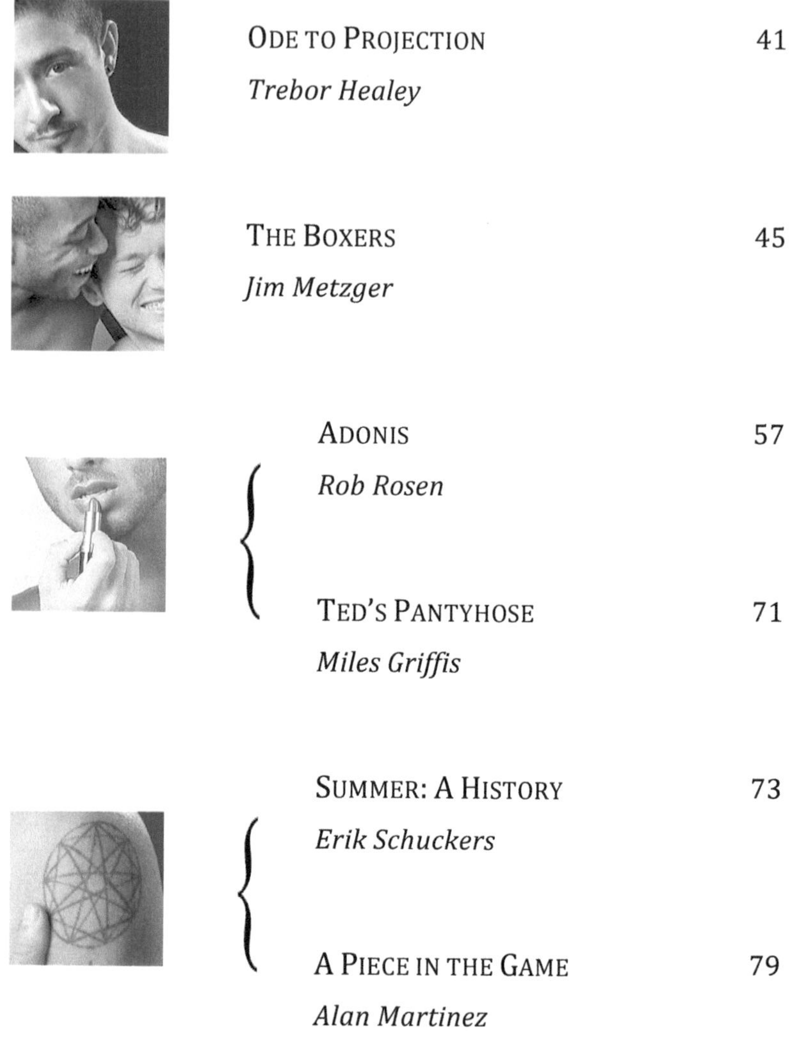

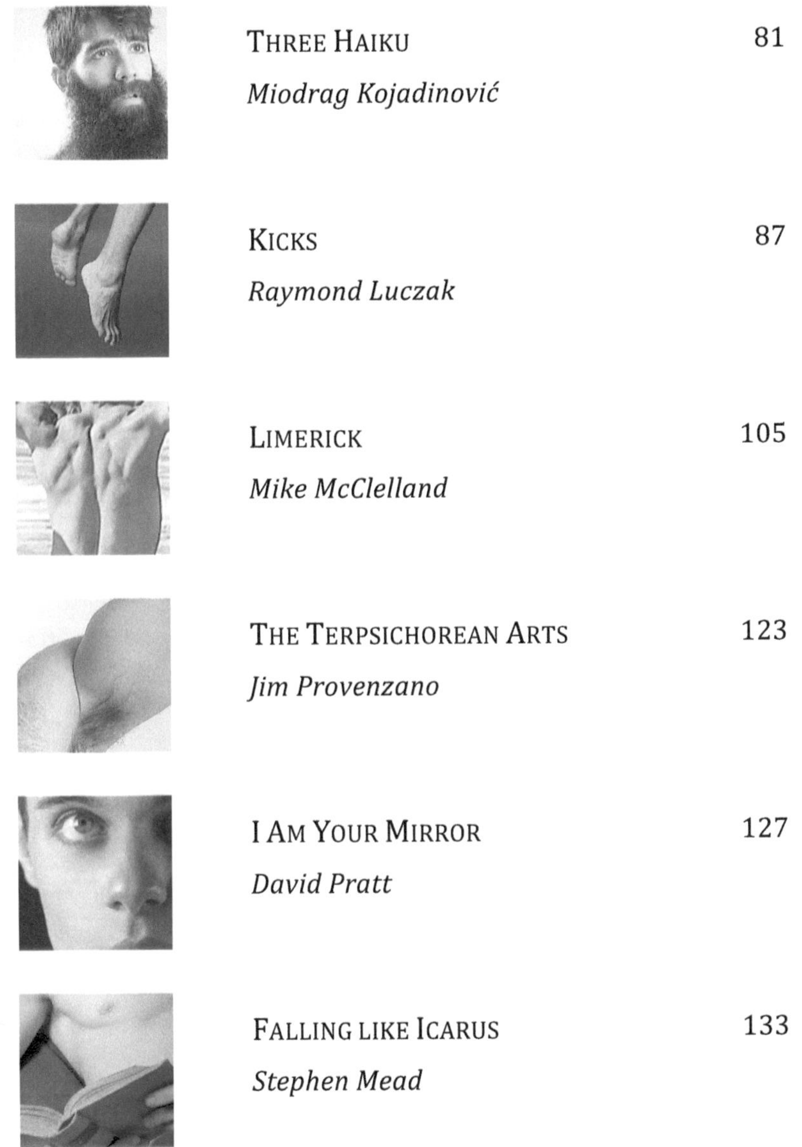

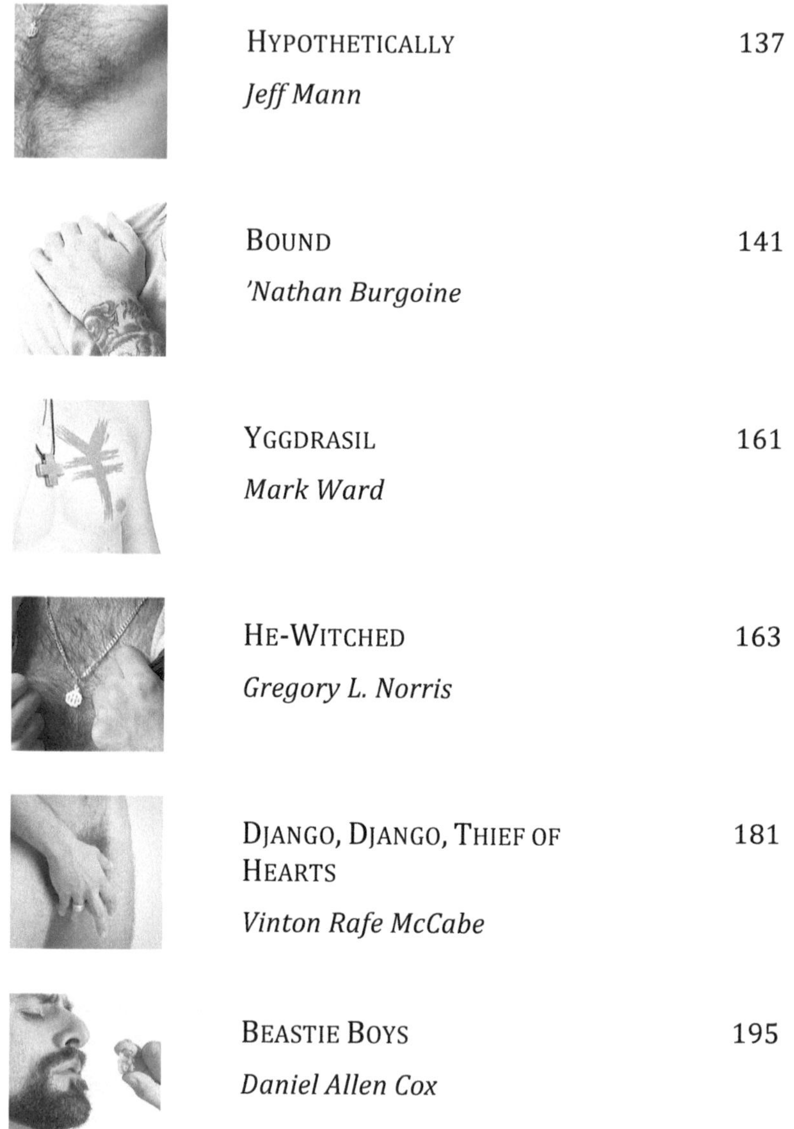

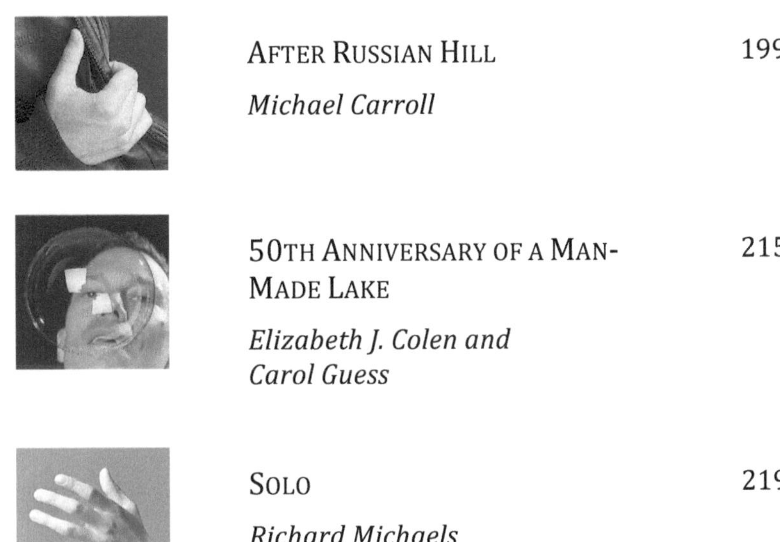

Introduction

There is no mystery to a go-go boy. Nothing could be more obvious, more frank. On a bar or stage, he is there to be looked at, to arouse our lust and thirst, to keep us rooted to the spot by suggesting we might, through some act of extravagance or stroke of luck, become part of his erotic world.

What if we could? And what if that world held more than meets the eye?

The photographs in this anthology move beyond the stereotype. They take the dancer from the dance, place him in a new context, and invite us to explore the unexpected. It's a risky business. Too often the results of such translation are disappointing, what Kirk Read calls "an endless array of tanned, starved, over-groomed bodies looking into the headlights of studio portraiture."

Those are not the kinds of photographs Dot takes. Taking his name from the pixel that is the basis of his art, Dot uses his digital camera to explore drag shows, beer busts, Burning Man, faerie gatherings, male escorts, and street people. The models shown here, though all go-go boys, vary widely in their backgrounds: moonlighting ballet dancers, graduate students working on their PhDs, sex workers, porn stars, artists trying to scrape together enough cash to make it in an increasingly gentrified city. Their poses are whimsical, haunting, satiric, playful, ominous. They are not mere icons, but stories waiting to be told.

The authors are a varied lot as well. There are award winners and first-timers, poets, playwrights, novelists, and essayists. Two are former go-go dancers; one has chosen to write about his own photo. Given the freedom to follow wherever the picture leads, they span genres and modes, producing innovations and juxtapositions: a hip-hop villanelle; a two-person one-act where a cell phone may be a hidden third character; a haunting lyric in which the murders of Allison Parker and Adam Ward play out on a television screen across the room.

There is magic in these stories, too—and trances and prophecies and at least one demonic mortgage broker. There are dancers with injured bodies and romantics with wounded hearts looking for healing. Some find it with the help of an insightful drag queen; a few get more than they bargained for. Aging and AIDS, addiction and disability also enter these worlds. The glossy surface harbors mysteries after all.

The photos link to the stories in different ways. Some stories lead up to the image we see at the start. In others, we leave the literal behind and the picture becomes metaphor, capturing the mood but only alluding to the action. We see what the dancer feels like on the inside, a yearning for contact, an echo of flight.

What ties these tales together? Only our projections and our willingness to discover what lies beneath. The authors take us far beyond the beat of the go-go bar into the charged intersection of expectation and reality. Their journeys all step off from a common platform: the surface of a photograph.

—Nevada City
February, 2016

Not Just Another

Pretty Face

Frontispiece

Louis Flint Ceci

The skin is where we start, it is the hook.
And who from supple surface would be spared?
Who wouldn't, by its cover, judge the book?

And even if it happens we mistook
A membranous embrace for one that cared,
The skin is where we start. It is the hook

That pierces pretense deep and can't be shook.
Unscathed, unplumbed are those who never erred,
Who never, by its cover, judged the book.

That man whose glance can make your bowels cook—
That's potent, though the moment goes unshared.
The skin is where we start; it is the hook.

Supposing for a moment you could look
Like him, would you protest, to one who dared,
"You shouldn't, by its cover, judge the book"?

Or would you offer all the flesh it took?
Wisdom burns where boundaries are bared.
The skin is where we start. It is the hook.
Go on: you've judged the cover. Buy the book.

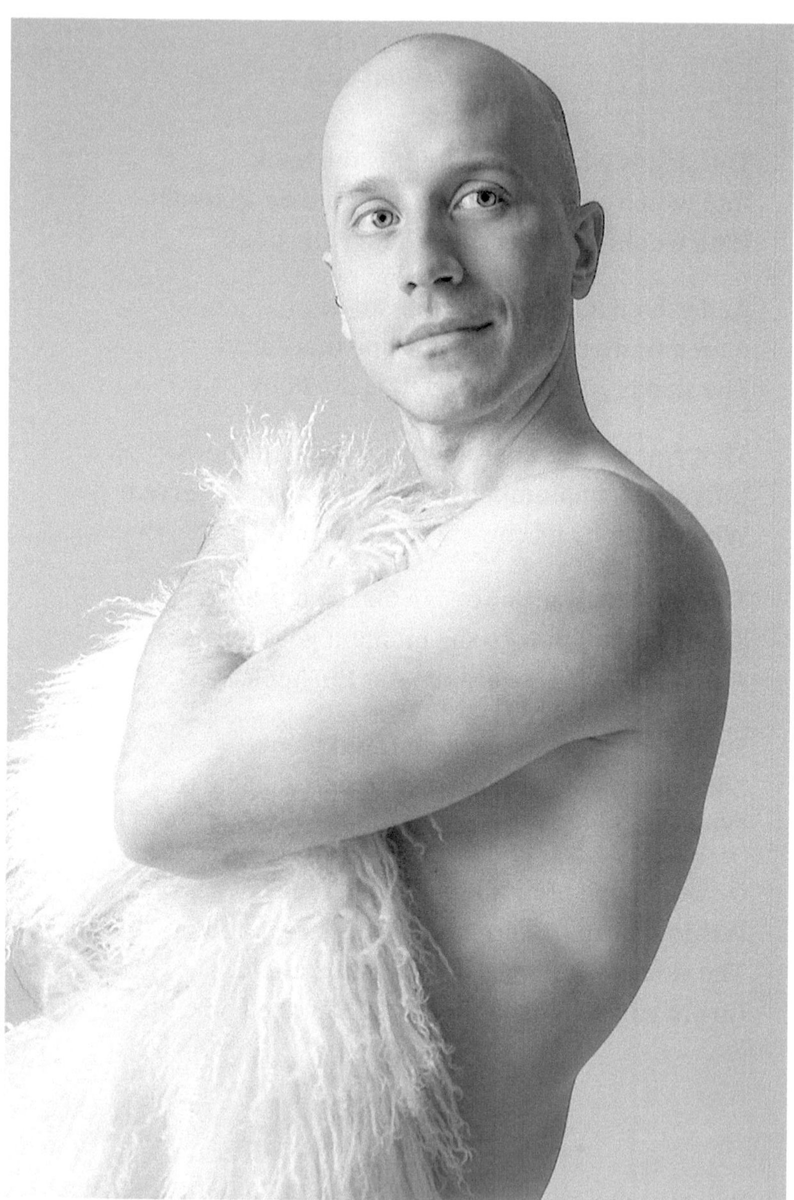

Your Pretty Little Head

Lewis DeSimone

1

Four people have already shared by the time I notice him. I would say I've been too busy focusing on them, but the truth is I can't tell you what they look like. I can't even tell you what they've said. It's all a murmuring jumble, like the adult voices in a Charlie Brown cartoon.

I must have spent the first half of the meeting with my head down, studying my fingernails. I've become obsessed with my fingernails lately, making sure they're just the right length all the way around the tip, and smooth, with no sharp edges to get caught on my clothes. And clean. They have to be clean. That's probably what I was doing while the others spoke—cleaning them. My nails used to be filthy, bits of paint lodged on their undersides, bits that I could never get to with soap and a nail brush. There was no point in cleaning them then; they'd only get dirty again the next day. It's harder to find any smudges now, but that doesn't stop me from looking. Now it's just the ink from a leaky pen, or a drop of mustard from lunch. I keep them all just long enough that I can slide one under its complement on the other hand and scoop out whatever remnants of the world have gotten stuck there. There's always something if I look closely enough. So that's probably what I've been doing while the others wail on about how long it's been since they last gave in to their addiction.

When I finally do turn my eyes away from my hands, I'm looking right at him. He's directly across the circle from me, sitting quietly, one leg crossed over the other at the knee, gently bouncing as if a doctor were tapping it with a rubber mallet.

But what I really notice, what I can't take my eyes from, is his bald head—perfectly smooth, like Yul Brynner's, shining in the overhead light. I stare at it, wondering if he has alopecia. I check his forehead for eyebrows and find the faintest blond caterpillars arching over his eyes. And then, the longer I look, I'm able to make out stubble here and there—around his ears, along the crown of his head—as if it's growing before my eyes. Which, I wonder, is growing—the hair or the sharpness of my vision?

Finally, he lifts his head, so that his eyes—an indecipherable color from this distance (only later will I learn they are a probing gray)—suddenly make direct contact with mine. And he smiles knowingly, as if he could tell all along that I'd been watching him.

The embarrassment of being caught brings me swiftly back into the room, into the moment. I turn away from the snare of his eyes and toward the sound of a throat clearing to my left, a woman's faint voice gaining strength awkwardly with each syllable she speaks.

"Hi," she says, "I'm Marilyn."

"Hi, Marilyn." Instant chorus, perfectly in synch. By the third share, the room always starts to click, like an a cappella group just getting their stride a few songs into the performance.

Marilyn tosses her head to one side, long red hair falling over one shoulder. Her legs, clad in skinny jeans, are perfectly aligned, angling back under the chair as though to hide her feet. "I'm a dancer," she says. "I haven't danced for six months." And then she lets out a soft giggle.

"Dancing was my life. I danced for years. Well, to be accurate, I *tried* for years. And I thought I was pretty good. Several people thought I was pretty good—friends. Or people who think complimenting you and encouraging hopeless dreams is the friendly thing to do. The people that really counted were less impressed. I can't tell you how many times I got rejected—how many auditions I had to skulk away from with my tail hiding in my tutu. But I kept coming back for more. You know what they say about insanity. Shuffle ball change, repeat." She attempts another smile but quickly thinks better of it.

Beside her, Jerry, the musician, beats an air drum solo. He keeps his hands close together, the gestures minimal, but whenever someone makes a dramatic point, I can see him hit his imaginary cymbals.

"I'm much happier now," Marilyn continues. "If you don't try, you can't be disappointed." She grimaces, as though searching for more words and finally realizing she has none. "Thanks for listening."

The chorus booms back mechanically. "Thanks, Marilyn."

2

Next up is James. James has shared at every meeting I've ever gone to, whether here at the community center, at the clinic near my office, or in the church basement across town. At first I thought he was following me, but after hearing his story a few times I realized he was just that desperate. God knows how many meetings he goes to that I've never even heard of. James needs a lot of help.

"Hi, I'm James," he says now, lifting his hand in a perfunctory wave. "I'm a writer."

"Hi, James."

"And I can tell you exactly how many rejections I've gotten. I printed them all out. I have a file drawer full of them. If I ever get the nerve, I'll have one hell of a bonfire."

I know James's story better than my own, so naturally my mind starts to wander again at this point. My new friend across the room must feel the same way. As I turn away from James, I spot that bald head shifting along with mine, and our eyes meet once more. His smile is sly this time, his lower lip scrunched to one side. He's probably heard James's story more than once, too.

3

After the last share, we meet by the refreshment table, sorting through the few items that weren't pillaged during the break. "Ken," he says by way of greeting, and extends a hand.

His fingers are long and soft, but his grip is firm. I find myself returning it with unaccustomed strength, lest my own fingers get crushed. Then again, I think, that might solve one problem. A hand that can't hold a brush is a hand that can't be tempted.

"I only came for the doughnuts," he says after I've introduced myself. He reaches across me and grabs a chocolate iced glazed with sprinkles.

"Too rich for me," I say, patting my belly. "I'm no longer as svelte as I used to be."

Ken nods. "I know what you mean. Metabolism's a bitch after 30. That's why I smoke."

I pull the lever on the coffee and watch it drip into my cup.

"You laugh," he says, "but it's true. All you can do is substitute one vice for another. The human body is a flawed thing. There's no perfecting it."

4

Ken doesn't have to tell me he's new to meetings. I can read it in his body language—the stiff expression that says he's trying hard to withhold judgment. I was pretty much the same in the beginning, cynical every step of the way, especially when it came to the Higher Power stuff. It's belief in a higher power that gets us into this crap in the first place, that higher power being inspiration.

We're walking down the darkened street, the first ones out the door. The regulars take their time moving on from the meeting, half of them clearly afraid to let go and rejoin the world. They typically go off somewhere for an informal session—more cross-talk, fewer rules—baby steps away from the twelve.

I tell myself Ken needs a sponsor, and I might be just the right fit. I've never been anyone's sponsor before. I can't believe these thoughts are even occurring to me. How can I possibly help someone else when I'm still struggling myself? Then again, maybe the effort to help someone is just the distraction I need.

Unless I'm kidding myself. Unless the only thing I really want to help myself to is his cock.

5

I'm a painter. It's been two years since I last picked up a brush.

"Are these all yours?" Ken asks, scanning the walls of my living room. Just over his head, a portrait of my brother stares back, black eyes probing. Beside him, enclosed by a distressed frame I found at a garage sale, is a landscape from a long-ago trip to Taos.

"Yes," I say, rushing past the paintings in pursuit of wine. I have a mini-cellar in the pantry, a rack that I like to organize meticulously so I can pick the right bottle even if the lights are out. The first column is Pinot Noir, followed by Merlot, Zinfandel, Cabernet—the richer bottles farther from the door, so you have to work for them.

A California Merlot is enough for tonight. I set a bottle on the counter and remove the cork with a satisfying plunk.

"They're good," Ken says, taking a glass and gesturing back to the wall.

"Not good enough," I say. I lift my glass in a silent toast to failure.

"Did you ever sell any?"

"A few. Now and then. A friend of a friend would occasionally ask me to do a portrait. Mostly, though, I would just paint what I wanted to paint. And not sell it, of course." I lead him back into the living room. Over the years, the paintings have come to seem like wallpaper to me; I know they're there but never have to notice them. But Ken is so interested, scoping out each one so carefully, I suddenly feel surrounded. Paint everywhere—memories, dreams. Accusations.

"What about you?" I ask, craving a change of subject. "What devil did you sign up with? Terpsichore? Calliope? Erato?"

He ducks his head. It takes a moment for a mischievous smile to curl its way onto his lips, for his eyes to open in Norma Desmond exaggeration. "I'm an actor," he says facetiously, two equally stressed syllables, the second rhyming with *more*.

"I can see it."

"Can you? Well, nobody else did." Pouring a refill, he says, "I blame my mother. She was obsessed with awards shows when I was a kid. I'd watch them all with her, and got completely obsessed with the glamour. I couldn't have been more than seven when I decided on my main goal in life: I was going to stand on that stage someday, with an Oscar in my hand, with millions watching."

"Did you like it?"

"Acting?" He gently squeezes his lower lip between long, white fingers. "Yeah. I loved it." He walks slowly toward me and gazes up at the portrait of my brother. I forgot how evil I made him look. "I played Edmund in *Long Day's Journey* once, in college. It was amazing. I've never felt more alive. Ironically, playing a man who wishes he were dead."

I don't have to ask the obvious question, why he quit. We all know why we quit our various rackets. We quit because the desire is always stronger than the payoff. We quit because it's less painful than continuing to try.

"What's in there?" he asks, gesturing toward the closed door near the kitchen. He asks like he already knows.

I don't bother answering, just open the door.

I haven't been inside the studio for months. There's still a canvas on the easel, a half-finished image I can barely remember. Other canvases, in various stages of development, lean against the walls. The room still smells of linseed.

Ken meanders through, dodging the canvases and tarps on the floor.

"What's your day job?" he asks, studying the image on the easel.

"I work at a bank."

"So what would you tell people at parties? When they asked what you did?"

The room suddenly smells like cyan blue. In reality, I know that all the paint colors smell alike, but after a while I developed a kind of sixth sense for them. I knew the scent of blue, the distinct sound of yellow.

"At first, I would say, 'I'm a banker, but I also paint.'"

Ken nods.

"Then, there was a time when I decided I was giving myself short shrift. I wanted to be known as a painter, so I changed it up. 'I'm a painter, but I make my living as a banker.'"

"Did that work better?"

"Not really. It sounded like I was making excuses."

"I see."

"So next, I got really bold. When someone asked, I would just say, 'I'm a painter.' That, at least, got the conversation going. The danger was that some people assumed I was famous. They'd ask question after question about where my work was hung, and I ran out of answers. Until this one guy put an end to it all. 'I'm a painter,' I said, and he just stared at me. 'But what do you do for money?' he asked."

"Ooh," Ken says, "a smart one. He was probably an artist, too."

6

He's back the next week, a little more comfortable, a little more open to the process. He even shares. My first share was one of the most terrifying moments in my life, blatant exposure in front of a room full of strangers. But Ken's an actor; he's used to that.

He had his last audition a few weeks ago. "It's been a year of rejections," he says. "And the last time, a little light went on in my head as I was leaving the room. More like a voice, actually. A voice inside my head that suddenly said, 'Why are you doing this to yourself?' At that moment, I knew it would be the last time. There's more to life than spilling my soul on stage to an unappreciative world. Fuck 'em."

There are a few titters around the room. People aren't quite used to the f-word's appearance in the middle of all the God references that weave their way into most speeches at these meetings. I, for one, breathe a sigh of relief. Ken's anger is refreshing. With that one word, he could be speaking for all of us. Fuck 'em, indeed.

7

Artists—even former artists—are definitely a breed apart. We're the only 12-step group in town that follows up each meeting with a few rounds at the bar.

Of course, the ringleader is James, the writer. His idol is F. Scott Fitzgerald.

"Pitchers all around!" he cries, calling the waitress over to our table.

The waitress, who's been working here for as long as I can remember, is in her late fifties, hair in streaks of gray and bottle blonde. She's hovering over Ken, who looks up at her and orders a whiskey.

"No no no!" shouts James, spreading his arms across the table as though to block a crowd of revelers. "Start slow, my friend, it's going to be a long night." He smiles at the waitress. "We'll have two pitchers of Guinness, please." He winks at Ken. "To start."

Paddy's Place is an institution in this neighborhood, and one of the longest-running establishments in town. The wood paneling has worn down over time, but the golden beer taps are gleaming. It has the cozy feel of an Irish pub—dark walls, low ceiling, tables a bit too close together. It's the sort of place Joyce himself might have gone to hoist a few.

"I liked your share tonight," James tells Ken. "You're quite right: time is too precious to waste it on art. Art is a distraction, my friends. It's a distraction from life." He raises his glass into the light, and the beer glows amber at the center.

Marilyn's in a more academic mood. "I don't agree," she says quite firmly. "Art is a *reflection* of life."

"Well," James allows, "it is that, of course. But I'm not talking about the result. I'm talking about the process. I had no idea how much time I was spending on it until the day I stopped. Suddenly, there were hours open to me, days, entire weekends. That was a new concept for me. Beforehand, weekends were simply an occasion for me to sit down for two solid days and write."

"But you enjoyed it, didn't you?" Ken asks. His voice is preternaturally soft, hesitant.

James throws his head back and breathes in a memory. "Oh yes," he says. "I loved it. Tinkering with a story, figuring out where it's going, what it's about, making the characters do my bidding, and inevitably discovering that they didn't give a damn what I wanted." He laughs. "I loved it. The way other people love cocaine."

"Or beer," I say, lifting my glass.

Everyone laughs heartily. I don't know if anyone at this table has a problem with alcohol, but if they do, god help them in this crowd. We're dealing with one addiction at a time.

8

Janet, the poet in the group, purses her lips. She's barely touched her beer. She hasn't said anything so far, but her eyes are always probing—observing, thinking. You get the feeling she's constantly processing, distilling ideas down to their essence. That's what poets do.

"I have a confession to make," she says at last. "I still write poems." She looks up and casts her eyes around the table, taking us all in. Her eyes are pale blue, so pale you have to squint to really see them. "The difference is that I don't send anything out anymore. I've changed my expectations. I think of it like needlepoint."

"Needlepoint?" I find myself giggling nervously.

"Yes," she says with a smile. "My grandmother used to do needlepoint. It was like meditation for her, something to pass the time while chatting with me or waiting for the roast to come out of the oven. She made pillows. Beautiful pillows, with wonderful patterns on them. And when she was done, she'd put the pillow on her bed or on the sofa. And there it was, this beautiful thing that gave her pleasure. She'd look at the pillow and you could see the pride in her eyes. Inside, I knew, she was saying, 'Isn't that pretty. I made that.' And friends would come over to the house and tell her what a pretty pillow it was. And she'd thank them, so pleased that they appreciated her work.

But she never picked up one of those pillows and marched into the street. She never held it over her head and barked to the world, 'Look what I made! Who wants to buy one?' She just did her work. And that was enough."

Janet draws a hand through her short-cropped hair, thin gray strands that hug her face. "That's how I think about all of it. The occasional kind words of someone who happens to see your work and appreciate it suffice. It's *your* needlepoint, *your* pillow. You make it for yourself. The real pleasure is in the doing—the needle pulling you through."

There's a long pause now, an awkward pause, as if there are limits to sharing even in this crowd.

"To needlepoint!" James calls out at last, breaking the silence with a glass held high in the air.

The rest of the group echoes the toast, some glasses clinking, others merely suspended aloft for a moment before coming back to the lip. Already, things aren't as orderly as they were when the evening began.

"Maybe," Ken opines, "that's the only way. Just give in to it in small doses."

"True," says James, "the addiction is always there."

I have to join in at some point. "Whether you're using or not," I remind them, "you're always an addict. Which means, James, you're always just a sentence away from writing another novel."

James puts down his beer to fully embrace the laugh that now ripples through him. "Just a sentence away."

"The problem," says Jerry, both forearms flat on the tabletop, as if he's grown tired of his imaginary drumming, "is that the only way to make any money is to prostitute yourself by doing what other people want instead."

"Unless you prostitute yourself the old-fashioned way," James says, "and sleep with someone with the power to get your best work out there."

"For some people," Jerry says, "that *is* their best work."

There are a few loud guffaws. James's voice arcs over them: "To prostitution!!"

9

The conversation goes around like this for a while. It always does. It's our way of processing, saying the things we can't say in the room, where we're expected to hew to Bill W's tenets. Here, at the bar, we can let off steam, but still under the protective eye of our peers, people who are just as invested in our artistic sobriety as we are. People who know just how far to let you go before reeling you in—stopping your hand from touching the brush, the pen, the keyboard (musical or electronic, depending on your particular poison).

But Ken is new to this game. He doesn't really know when to quit. "How do you keep the temptation away?" he asks. "I mean, we're all expressive types. We live to express ourselves."

And suddenly, he's standing beside the table. As his hips begin to sway, I grow aware of the music. Bar music is usually just background noise to me, and I'm not terribly familiar with anything written since 1990. But the song playing at the moment is one of the biggest hits of the year, a funky beat that even I find infectious. Ken's body is moving with it, snakelike swirls from his feet up to his shoulders. The song is overtly sexual, and his hips know it.

The others start clapping along to the beat, encouraging him. He steps onto his chair and continues to swirl. It's only another moment before he's on the tabletop, feet planted next to the beer pitcher. The others move their glasses out of the way to give him room.

The whole bar is watching now. I have an eye out for the bartender, ready for him to march over and pull Ken off the table. But instead he just watches. Meanwhile, Ken goes on, grooving, trancelike, a smile bursting onto his face, the curve of his lips an inverse of the line that defines the top of his head.

Cheers erupt from various spots in the bar. Acknowledging them, Ken slowly peels off his t-shirt, revealing smooth skin, subtle striations of abs. His jeans are hung low, revealing the elastic of his underwear, a thin trail of hair peeking out below his navel.

In another bar, I think, his briefs would already be stuffed with dollar bills.

10

There was a time when I invited men up to see my etchings. Without irony.

Now it's Ken who leads me up the stairs. "I want you to paint me," he says.

"Paint you?" I ask in a low voice—the way most people would react if someone asked you to buy them heroin. I'm having a hard time getting the key in the lock, my fingers as befuddled as my head. I finally realize I've been holding it upside down.

"Paint you?" I repeat as the door finally swings open. "What are you talking about?"

"I think you need to paint again," he says, and casts me a look of brazen nonchalance.

"I don't paint. I can't."

"Why?"

"Because it's bad for me," I say. I'm already at the fridge, pulling out a bottle of Pinot Gris.

"Why?" He's like a toddler, relentlessly tossing the most annoying question my way.

"It gets my hopes up." The cork gives way suddenly, and the bottle rattles on the countertop.

"That's just it," he tells me. "It's like Janet said. You need to separate the art from the expectation. Don't hope for the work to lead to something. Just let it flow. Let it be."

"Easier said than done," I retort, giving him a hefty pour.

"Okay, I'll make a deal with you. Just give the painting to me. No worries about whether it's going to sell, or how good it is. Just give it to me. You'll never have to see it again, you'll never have to wonder." His bald head is pink from the cold, the color highlighting the smooth curve of his scalp.

It takes the rest of the bottle and a half hour of persistence to persuade me. By the time I set a blank canvas on the easel and pull out the tubes of paint, I can't remember any of his arguments, or my own. As Ken settles into position on a chair in the corner of the studio, I realize it's his face that won the debate—the soft gray eyes, framed by lascivious lashes, the smile that exposes just a hint of white teeth.

11

The tubes of paint feel hard, foreign in my hand. The white coating is cracked in the spot where each tube starts to roll, revealing the metallic surface beneath. Slowly, I squeeze out tiny cylinders of cadmium yellow, cerulean blue, alizarin crimson. The boldness of the pure color, unblended, shocks me for a moment. I'd forgotten what paint looks like in the raw, each hue whole to itself, unblemished by contact with others, spared the diffusion that comes with being absorbed into a thirsty canvas. I hesitate to mix it, to bastardize the red and blue into the precise shade of purple I need to reproduce Ken's diaphanous shirt. Finally, I swirl the colors together, birthing something new, something unique. It's impossible to reproduce a shade identically each time; it's all about the proportions, the degree of thoroughness in the mixing. It's never twice the same, and it's never quite the same as real life. Even those artists who crave verisimilitude know it's a myth. I have control in this moment—the freedom to add more of this, subtract some of that—but in the end, the paint itself will do what it wants.

I look up, just above the edge of the canvas and across the room, to where Ken sits, self-consciously still. Clearly, he's never posed before. He doesn't know what to do with his hands, where to turn his head. Like every first-time model, he assumes there's a right way to sit, a right way to be.

"Just look off to the side," I say. "One hand on the back of the couch, the other in your lap." I don't really care where he puts his hands, where he directs his eyes. But he needs to know. He needs to think it matters. He needs to believe the art cares.

My own eyes flicker back and forth, from the curve of Ken's head to the blank white of the canvas. I dip the brush into a pool of brown-black for the gentle outline of his head, and stand quietly for a long moment, deciding where to place the first line, the focal point from which the rest of the painting will emerge. I settle on the spot—a third of the way down from the top; that's where his head will start. The hand in his lap will mark the bottom margin. As the brush approaches the canvas, my hand begins to tremble, as if the bristles and the fabric have matching polarities, the one sent into a neurotic dance by the other. I take in a deep breath and will my hand to obey.

It requires a quick gesture—trusting the movement—and suddenly, as though drawn by an unseen hand, the semicircle of Ken's head appears before me on the canvas. The beginning. It begins. I am officially off the wagon.

When I look again at Ken—the real one, the flesh-and-blood man on the other side of the room—he's smiling, as if he sees something that pleases him, something new, something he's never seen before.

After a few minutes of hesitation, crafting an outline, proportions, picking just the right color here and there, the thinking seems to stop. It's as if I'm looking down from a corner of the ceiling, watching the model, the artist, the canvas that stands between them, as if it's not my hand that's making the connection, connecting life to art, making something of nothing.

I watch as the canvas comes to life—layers of color lending contrast and depth to each section of the image. The shirt is almost violet under the arm, but a bright lilac on the pocket, where the light hits it. And Ken's face goes from the uniform pink of a cartoon to the gradual shading of flesh.

The eyes are the last detail before I call it quits for the night. I mix a blend of black and white, but it gazes dully back at me from the canvas—lifeless, flat. Only when I add in a slight touch of blue does the gray take shape. I learned long ago that you can't really re-create the world as it is on a flat surface. It has to be changed in order to look real. It has to obey the rules of art in order to feel at all like life.

"Well?"

Ken's voice pulls me out of my reverie and I realize that I've been standing there for minutes, brush in the air like Bette Davis's cigarette holder, lost in the world of the picture. I'm suddenly aware of the smell of paint. It's everywhere now—wafting off the canvas, the table, my clothes.

"Can I see it?"

I smile, put the brush down, and pull myself away to make room for Ken to come around.

He peers at the canvas for a long moment before speaking. "That doesn't look anything like me," he says at last, and we both laugh.

"Yes it does," I say, pointing. "Look at the shape of the nose. That is totally you."

"You mean the pig snout? Thanks, hon." He turns back toward me, a playful look in his eyes, and I see the two together, Ken's head beside its reimagined self on the canvas. He's right, of course: on the surface they look nothing alike. And yet, the painting captures something I've never consciously noted before. On the canvas, there's a glow coming off him, as if something on the inside is pushing its way out. Only now, when he's standing there, next to his doppelganger, can I see it in Ken's eyes—the same glow, drawing me in.

12

I can't tell who moves in first. We meet somewhere in the space between us, lips opening and pressing against flesh, arms stroking arms, legs fitting together like jigsaw pieces.

There's no time to make it across the room to the sofa. Instead, we fall gently to the floor and enter a swirl of limbs and lips. I tear off my oil-reeking clothes and meet his flesh with my own.

Ken flips me over, onto my back. Behind and above him, the wall of portraits gaze down at me—faces I've known, tried to capture in two dimensions. Their eyes seem lifeless now, as if the paint on the canvas has suffocated them over time. A series of dead faces, watching.

My leg is twisted beneath me. I straighten it out, and it hits something. And in the distance, beyond my line of vision, I hear the easel crash to the floor, brushes clattering, something rolling toward a stop by the wall. I smile as Ken's face hovers above mine, the eyes alive, seeing me as I am, the round head shining so smooth I can almost see myself in its curve.

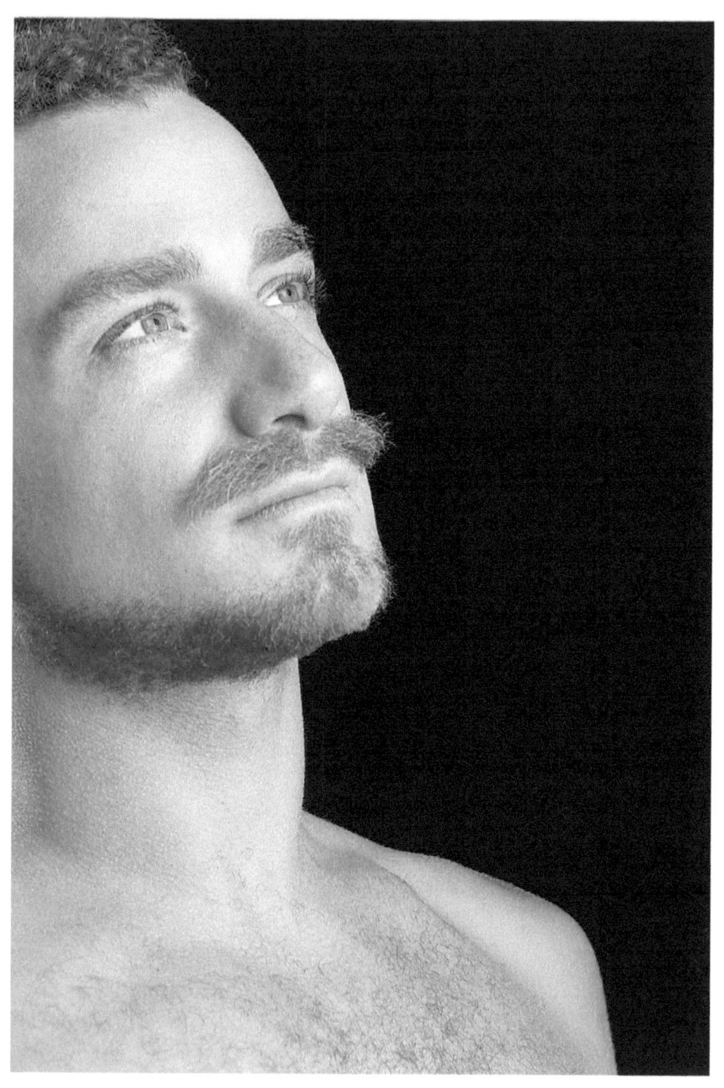

For Love and Resistance

Richard Wilde Lopez

I'm standing shirtless at this bar off 1st and 2nd Avenue painfully aware of how sticky the floor is. I don't know why I'm here but I can't seem to bring myself to leave. That rude perfume of sex keeps me planted to the gluey floor and I sip my second whiskey slowly surveying the situation. It's almost 1 a.m. and the party is picking up. New York, the nocturnal city: in its darkest hours the boys will play. Now I'm resisting the pull of the back room, the scent of poppers is in the air and I know my resistance is wearing thin. I should leave, go home, jerk off to some obscure amateur Internet porn and call it a night. I shoot the rest of my drink and I'm headed for the door when I look up and see a dark-haired boy wearing nothing but a backwards baseball cap and a white jock strap climbing up onto the bar. He's beautiful, strikingly so and I find myself walking a bit closer for a better look, my sticky shoes no longer an issue.

He's just getting started and I watch him as he finds his rhythm to the music. His eyes are closed and he's holding onto the sprinkler pipe attached to the ceiling for balance. He drops his body and lets his arms carry his weight. His torso is stretched long allowing the musculature of his body to be viewed in full. Each sculpted square of his abdomen glows under the red bar lighting. Other men have begun taking notice of him.

I'm staring now, embarrassed that I've become one of the go-go boy gawkers, but I can't help myself. You see, I've always had this habit of staring. Of course he's designed to entice. I know the deal. Every twist and turn he makes, every little smirk and wink intended to lure you in with a false promise: You can have me, his face says, touch me, his body beckons, but his eyes betray him. This is just a job, no matter how much fun he is having; there is no intention for love. His attention is yours for just one moment and another dollar, it is a dirty ruse and that is the truth about a go-go boy. The other men are pushing bills into his jock strap. I will not be one of them.

I do however have this strange urge to take him off that bar. I want to bring him home and make him dinner. I want to touch his face and smell his hair. I do not pity him nor do I shame him; no, it's not that simple. I yearn for him and I'm shocked by my thoughts. I'm having a full-blown fucking fantasy. In my head I've made this boy love me. We hold hands in the street and he charms my friends with his humor and good looks. He reads poetry and loves jazz. Our sex is rough and wet but passionate, the look-into-my-soul kind of sex. I find myself getting hard as I imagine licking the sweat off this boy's abs.

"Girl, you got it bad."

"Excuse me?" I turn to see a painted white face with dark blue eye shadow dusted onto her lids. She's wearing a pink polka-dotted nun's habit and lime-green glittering false lashes.

"I was watching you stare at that dancer boy with your mouth open. You've got good taste, you should talk to him." She tucks a condom into my pocket and pats me on the ass with a rough push toward the bar. I'm annoyed but I walk toward him anyway.

The boy is dancing above me. I could see each of his sneakers straddling my head, black and white high tops, short socks. His dusty brown leg hair travels the length of his thighs and over his ass; damn I love a fuzzy ass. I want to touch his leg, he's so close I can smell the sweetness of his sweat like toasted sugar and musk. I reach out to stroke his leg and there's a white chubby hand petting his calf like a puppy. My hand retreats and I turn to see a piggish middle-aged bald white guy smiling ear-to-ear stroking the boy's leg. Between the black leather of his harness the man's skin bulges tight and pink with a shine to it that looks like he's coated in honey. He reminds me of this john I once had a few years ago. The guy liked to watch me shower while he jerked off. He had that same thin but tight pink skin as the man touching the dancer boy. I have this moment of nausea but it quickly subsides and I order a drink at the bar so I don't seem strange and I walk back over to my corner.

"You didn't even try, darlin'. What happened?"

"He's not really my type."

The boy looks me dead in the face as I say this. It's like he could hear me from across the loud bar. I know he can't, there's no way, but he holds my eyes and I feel myself blushing and I know I'm lying.

"You look at him with love, honey, and if there's one thing I can recognize in this whole fucked-up world is a man who knows how to love." I'm annoyed now. Who the hell does she think she is to tell me about love?

"My apologies, darlin'. I forgot to introduce myself. My name is Sister Fiesta Résistance, one of the Sisters of Perpetual Indulgence, the New York chapter." She smiles wildly at me and for a second I'm taken aback. There's not a tooth in her head! She's all shining pink glossy gums and I can't help but stare. In her makeup she is the stuff of nightmares. Little children would cry at the sight of her. Hell I'd cry right now if I weren't so drunk.

"Thirty-two."

"Thirty-two what?"

"Teeth, peanut. Thirty-two teeth extracted."

"Oh, I didn't mean to stare, it's a terrible habit. I'm sorry."

"Oh don't worry your little head, peanut. Habits are something I understand. Habits require particular circumstances to overcome them. You see I wasn't always the divine beauty that stands here before you." She does a little twirl, her gums like wet red plastic. "I used to be in luuuuv with Ms. Tina. She was my one true friend. My reason to live and all that I cared for. She was my savior from a terrible unjust world full of assholes and bigots. Now you see, I'm a very sensitive person, darlin'. I have many many feelings all the time. But sensitive people have no business with drugs, sensitive people need purpose or they succumb to their vices."

"Okay so thanks for sharing, but I'm gonna . . ."

"Excuse me! I'm trying to teach you an important life lesson here so you better sip your damn drink and listen." I put the straw to my lips and sip deeply.

"Children have no patience these days. Fuck. Now I need a shot." She makes me wait and makes a show of ordering two shots of whiskey. The cocktail boy looks very uncomfortable as she slips a five-dollar bill into his jockstrap and jumps slightly when her long fingernails graze the base of his dick. I stare at the boy on the bar and notice he has a bruise on his right butt. It makes him cuter to me for some reason and that urge to take care of him tightens. I wonder how he got this bruise. Did he slip off the bar? Did someone hurt him? Is it a sex wound? We down the shots and Sister Fiesta Résistance shudders dramatically.

"Whoa, Mama can't take a shot the way she used to," she says, dabbing her lips with a handkerchief like a proper lady. "Okay so where was I. Oh yes, so I was addicted, honey. And I don't mean a dabble here or there, I was riding that dark wave straight through the veins." She pulls up her sleeves and shows me her track marks. "I remember even thinking there was no way I would ever consider loving someone who wasn't also into crystal. Dreams of meth-head love, if you will." She chuckles at this past thought but a part of me understands what she means: when you hold something inside that you find so dark that you can't ever imagine anyone accepting you. You can't envision ever being loved except through this shared darkness. I understand darkness.

"And then I met a man. Isn't it always a man, darlin'? A beautiful man named Robert. Robert had the most beautiful smile, like a Colgate commercial or some shit. He was tall and handsome and the kindest man I've ever met. He liked fancy cheeses and dark beer and had a lab named Smudge. Let me tell you girl, any man that has a dog and can down a draft always gets me. When he smiled at me in that dark dark time of night and I felt his body heat as he pulled me into that beautifully hairy chest, I knew I had to be a better person. So I quit, cold turkey and I was happy, in love."

"And this Robert, he broke your heart, didn't he? He left you and destroyed what was left of your hopes and dreams, and now you're telling me some 'it's better to have loved and lost' bullshit, aren't you?"

"Well damn girl, aren't you a little too young to be pessimistic?"

"I'm a New Yorker, we're all pessimistic."

"Well, some people need to get the hell out of this city before their auras turn black black black as night. This city can turn even the brightest auras dark, honey, believe me. I've seen its destructive powers and they are masterfully effective. But anyway, you're half right, he did break my heart. He broke my heart the day he stepped onto Sixth Ave and was mowed down by a yellow cab. Bam! Just like that he was gone and I was devastated, left only with a Smudge."

I don't know what to say so I just sip my drink, letting the straw fill the gap between my mouth and the words that should be coming out of it.

"Oh honey, don't look so forlorn, your silence is drama drama drama! It was years ago. But a story never ends with death now, does it?"

"So what did you do? How did you deal?"

"Well I ran right back into the arms of the only friend I knew that could help me with my anguish, of course. I shut myself in my little apartment on Avenue B and let Ms. Tina medicate me with the sweet sweet fire that engulfed my grief and sent me straight on a course to Junky Town. I didn't eat, I barely slept and I let any disgusting man that wanted to crawl on top of me use my body for their sick pleasures. And why not, I was just a body now; my soul had gone when my Robert left this world. And I wanted nothing more than to join him. I need a cigarette, you smoke darlin'?"

We make our way to the door and I can feel the dancer's eyes watching me. I turn to see him smile right at me. I smile back feeling my face fill with blood and I realize how drunk I actually am. Outside the air is crisp, fall is here and I welcome the cool night air on my shirtless torso.

"Now where was I?" she says while exhaling her minty smoke. "Yes, I was a fucking mess."

"But you're clean now, right?"

"What a ghastly word. Clean. It implies too much purity. And honey, ain't none of us pure."

She's right. I hate the word, too, and I can't believe I used it. It causes shame and opposing hierarchies: those who are clean, and those who are unclean, dirty. I've left the beds of men who asked me, "Are you clean?"

"I'm sorry, you're right, it's a shitty word. What I meant was, how did you stop using?"

"No worries, doll. I can tell a sincere apology when I hear one." She takes another drag and looks me up and down as if she understands something more about me in that moment, like she's unraveled a little secret about me. I look down at my feet and take another drag of my own cigarette. I don't like to be looked at, especially this way.

"The day I stopped using, I was getting ready for a bath. I filled the tub right to the brim and let the bubbles get all fluffy, the foam raised in soft little peaks. I scented the water with rose oil and lit no less than one hundred votives, for effect. It was quite romantic. You see, I was tired of this world, all of it, and I wanted to leave feeling cleansed of its grime. I intended this to be my final departure from the world. My swan dive. This fabulous bubble bath with perfect lighting was to be my portal to the afterlife."

"You were going to commit suicide?"

"Oh yes, honey. I felt I had nothing left. My lover was gone. I had destroyed my good looks with crystal meth and degraded my body. No one wants to love a rotten-toothed junky with a broken heart. So I wrote my melancholy goodbye letter to the world, I thanked Judy Garland for her preciousness, and filled my syringe with a lethal dose, placing it ceremoniously on the closed toilet lid next to my tub. I stripped down naked and dipped into the sweet scalding water. I scrubbed myself raw, every inch, and let the water burn away my sins. I held the needle to my vein and took a look around the bathroom. The lighting was truly spectacular, flickering, and alive. Smudge was staring at me disapprovingly with a tilted head and that one upturned ear. But something was off. He knew it, too. The scene wasn't perfect just yet and it occurred to me that what was needed was a little soundtrack. So I put the needle down and went to retrieve my turntable. Being the dramatic Queen I am, I wanted the haunting voice of the great Nina Simone to carry me off into the nether world. I envisioned them finding my body in a beautiful tub encased in candle wax, Nina softly singing for the departed. It was a very classy affair."

She gazes into the traffic, present with her memory, telling me something personal. In my drunkenness I feel privileged to listen to these words. I stare at her. Even through her makeup I can see the pain it causes to relive this moment. I'm jealous of her ability to be this open, this exposed. People often seem to want to uncurl themselves around me like flowers ready to reveal their rawest parts. I prefer to be the one who watches, the voyeur. There's vulnerability in being watched, in showing someone the hidden parts. She's strong, like the dancer on the bar, nakedly encouraging others to look at him. I could never be that strong, I would wither into my shame.

"Now I must have been in a completely hypnotic state of determination to make this the most perfect suicide ever that it didn't even occur to me that I was dripping wet and barefoot. When I reached to plug in the record player with my soapy wet hand I shocked myself dead."

"Dead? What do you mean dead?" I ask in disbelief lighting a second cigarette.

"Dead, honey, deceased, no longer with us." She flicks her cigarette effortlessly into the street. "May I have one of yours? This menthol is killing me."

I hand her my lit cigarette and light a new one for myself.

"Thank you, babe. Let me tell you, sugar, being dead is nothing like you see on cable. There is no bright light, no gates of heaven, just blackness. But I was still around, that essence of what was truly me, and there was something else. I was not alone, my dear. I felt him all around me, crawling up my arms and out of my mouth and like a cold breath it gave me chills. And then I heard him as clear as day. 'Mark,' he said. My boy name is Mark, darlin'," she says, clutching my arm. "'Mark!' he called. It was Robert. My Robert! I could feel him smiling at me. I couldn't see him but I felt his bright beautiful smile. And you know what he said to me? He said, 'Mark. Don't be an idiot, open your eyes.'"

"Your man, the love of your life, came through from the other side to call you an idiot?"

"Oh yes honey, he used to call me an idiot all the time when he was alive: 'You idiot, your lip-gloss melted all over my favorite shirt in the dryer.' 'Damn it Mark, stop buying six-dollar lattes, we gotta pay rent, you idiot.' The man always kept me in check.

"Well anyway, my roommate had come home early from work and found me dead and naked on my tiled floor and called 911. The next thing I remember I was opening my eyes to see a rather handsome paramedic surrounded by the most beautiful golden light. It was his aura and it felt like for the first time I actually truly looked at someone since Robert was with me.

"After the incident I've been blessed with the gift of sight. My eyes had been opened. Now, if a certain person has a particularly strong energy about them, I can see their glowing force, their aura. Which leads us back to you, darlin'."

She is looking right at me and I wonder if she can see my aura. Is it tainted like my blood? Is it contaminated with deadly pathogens? Is it the gray color of fear and regret?

"Come, give me your palm."

I give her my hand and she traces the lines.

"Your health line has been interrupted but then extends for a very long time. You're healing, getting over something big that's changed you. I have to wait for them to heal before I get the new porcelain ones."

She says this sliding her tongue over her exposed gums.

"Isn't porcelain just the prettiest word? Look, dear, we all have to heal before we get what we want, but we can't heal alone. When I saw you I felt your sadness. It's all over your aura in tones of purple and mauve. But at its core there's a brilliant silvery blue. Don't let secrets darken that spirit."

She's right, and in that moment I feel calm and strong.

"Okay now, go right along inside and talk to that sexy dancer boy before someone snatches him up." She kisses me right on the cheek and I head for the door. I make my way through the crowd of shirtless men and walk over to the bar. The dancer boy smiles when he spots me. He crouches down to my level when I reach him.

"I thought you'd gone. I was getting worried I missed my chance to talk to you." His smile is beautiful and genuine and for the first time I get a good look at his face. He's even more handsome close up, short stubble and that lush dark hair I want to run my fingers through, strong jaw line. His eyes are kind and deep, his lashes are thick and long.

"I'm William," I say with my hand extended.

"Ari," he says, grasping my hand. He doesn't shake it, but he gives it a hard squeeze and pulls me closer to his face.

For a moment I get nervous he's going to kiss me but his lips reach my ear and I feel his breath on my face, I can smell him, musky sweetness.

"You're beautiful, William."

Before I can respond the bartender shouts last call and the guy behind me bumps me hard. I trip forward and knock over a glass, breaking it while trying to grab the bar for support.

"You're bleeding, William." I look at my finger and a red line of blood drips off the tip and onto the bar top. Ari holds my hand tightly and brings it to his mouth.

"No, don't!" I say a little harshly but he doesn't let go. He looks right into my eyes and sucks the blood off my bleeding finger.

He says, "That doesn't scare me," and winks. And I know he understands why I pulled away, why I always pull away. And in that instant I feel my resistance give way to possibility.

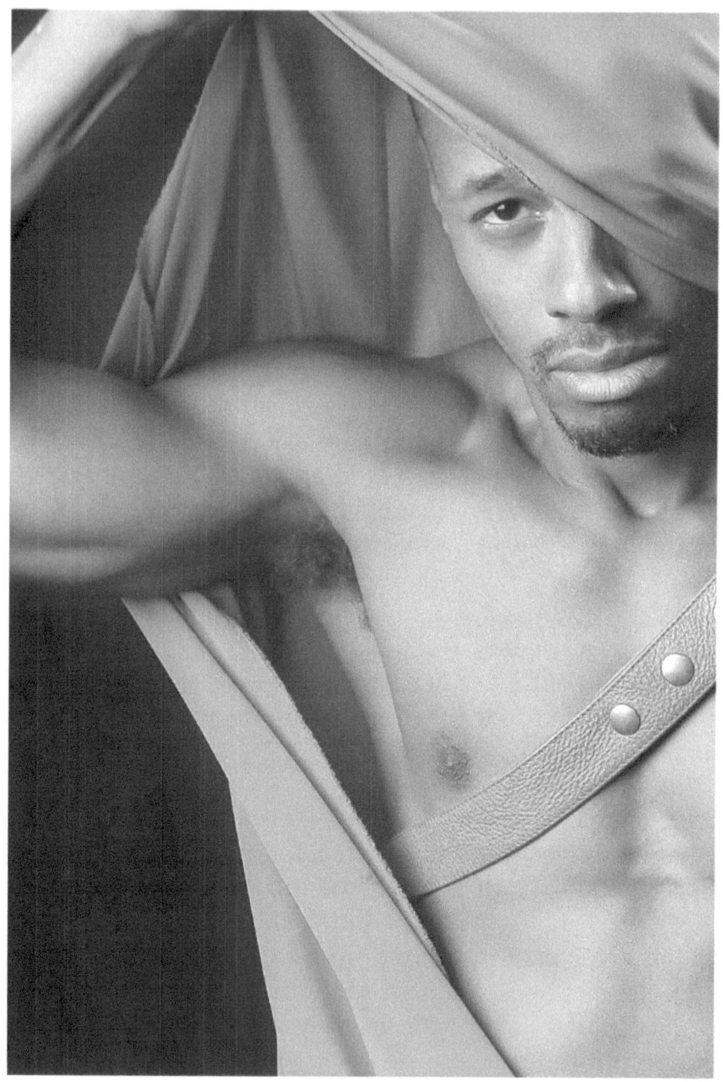

[AND WHEN WE TALK ABOUT HIS HANDS]

Johnathan Lay

under the lights fearful eyes bend
and build fantasies as large and fragile as sandcastles
broken on the shores of mouths

with a little sleek pill atop his head
he does a little dance for daddy
gyres and woofs and yaws and moans and maws
    a thank-you

for the hard-earned tangled in elastic
for the eyes that think a dollar worth the show
for the desperate grab of admiration in his jock

his hips wave and they wait with crumpled bills
for him to break across their shore
a smooth pivot and he counts the lust washed out to sea

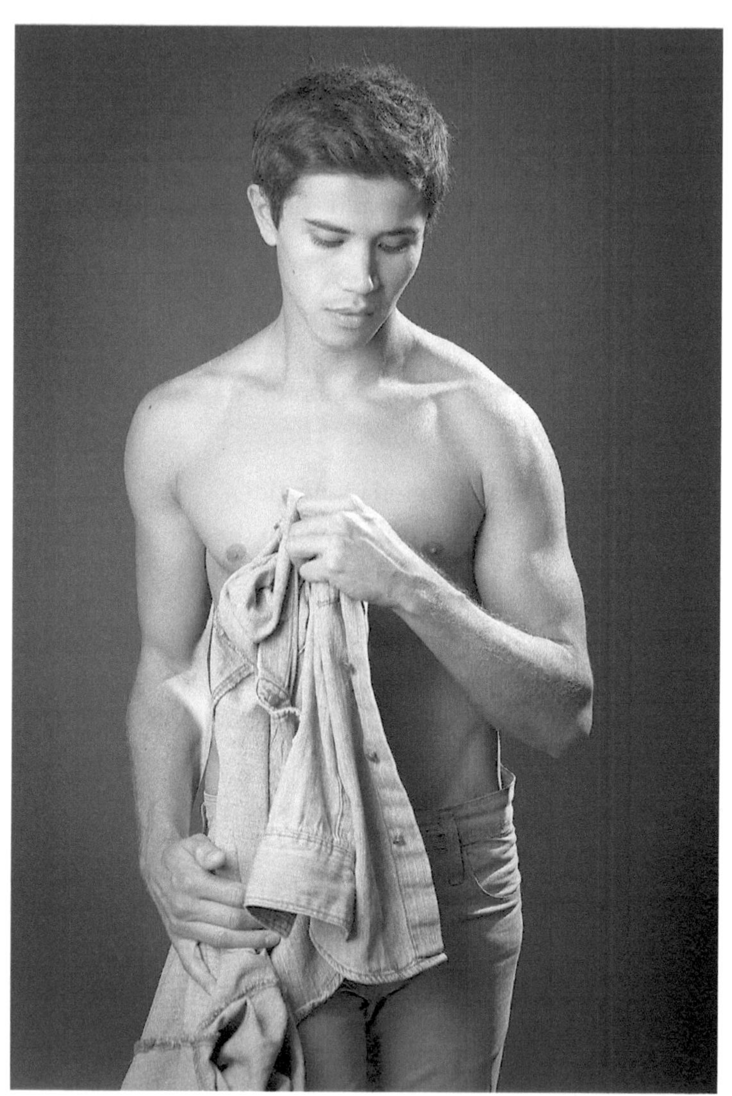

Packing

Salome Wilde

I've always enjoyed packing a suitcase. Weekend getaways are my favorite, choosing my clothes carefully so I bring the bare minimum for maximum impact. Dress slacks and shirts and socks and shoes first, then fitted t-shirts and cargo shorts, four of my favorite pairs of snug briefs, and whatever casual shoes meet the occasion and weather—sneakers, loafers, or sandals. Of course, I modify based on whether it's a solo adventure, fun with friends, or a romantic rendezvous. And I enjoy all equally, particularly in a busy life where free weekends are a rarity.

"Not *those* again," Paolo groans.

Though he's being overly dramatic, I accept the complaint. The skimpy turquoise tan-through swim suit is old and worn, but it's my favorite. Looks damn good on me, if I say so myself. But to Paolo, it's a reminder of impermanence. He knows I've worn it on many a trip, and on those trips I slept around. Neither of us doubts I'm likely to sleep around again, even if I'm committed to our relationship for right now. Sometimes I'm monogamous, sometimes I'm not, but I don't cheat. And I won't on Paolo, that's for sure. I don't know how it'll end, but we both went through a decent dose of shit when we were younger, and I'll do a lot to avoid hurting him again.

I roll my eyes, toss the suit back in the drawer, and pull out the green surfer shorts with the white hibiscus print. I bought them on my one and only trip to Florida, a sun-drenched Miami vacation with a rich guy who didn't allow me to pack a thing. I look them over. I don't entirely hate them. Paolo nods approvingly as I fold them and drop them into the case.

He rises from his viewing position on my bed. We're both naked, that preference being another thing we have in common. As usual, he's hard. He smiles through his crooked front teeth, a feature many men find endearing. "You look good in everything, Duc," he says smoothly, using the Vietnamese name I never do anymore and pronouncing it badly. The language doesn't fit his Mediterranean-American mouth, though my cock does, and soon he's on his knees proving it.

"I'm trying to pack," I complain, but it's half-hearted. Looking down as Paolo noses my balls then licks up from the base to the tip of my cock, I can't help but meet his grin and rise to the occasion. I thread my fingers into his thick, shaggy mop of black curls and push him down. He takes me in and I moan at the familiar warmth of his lips and tongue. But we have business to take care of if we're going to get to Santa Monica before dark, and I want to get going. After a few bobs, I groan, "Come on, Trouble," pulling him off my dick with an audible pop. "We have a six-hour drive ahead of us."

He frowns as he rises, the pout making him look younger than he is. Youthful appearance is another similarity between us. We draw big tips from those who like the "exotic" pretty-boy look. I get some of my looks from Ba, but it's mixed-race Ma who gets the credit for my boyishness. She looked too young to marry my father when they met in their early twenties. By the time I hit puberty, Ma and I looked more like siblings than mother and son—a fact that creeped me out entirely and brought tons of unwanted attention. In restaurants, servers would assume we were both Ba's kids. At the movies, people would look at us like we were a couple. And the guys at school hit me with offensive bullshit from every direction. While I was desperately trying to sort out a bi-racial bilingual gay identity in WASPy small-town southern Illinois, they were doing all they could to make it impossible. Cracks ran the gamut from "Your mom's kinda hot; why'd she marry your chink dad?" to "I bet your dad fucks you by mistake sometimes."

Paolo catches me in the past and ruffles my hair to bring me out of it. "Get your bathroom bag," he says, his hard-on pointing the way.

I toss my head and nod. "Bathroom bag." It's mostly ready, packed with whitening toothpaste and travel toothbrush, electric razor, comb, and a spare set of contacts just in case. I open the linen closet and reach for an unopened pack of condoms, thinking of all the places sand can get. I shiver with pleasure. The tiniest part of my brain wonders if Paolo is "the one." I push the idea away as I drop the condoms in and zip the bag shut. Then I pause to give myself a once-over in the mirror. I give a cheesy smile, which immediately summons my usual wish that I were square-jawed and sexy instead of "ethnic" and cute. I smack my flat belly as I leave, a reminder not to let Paolo talk me into too much rich, fatty food while we're on the beach. As I'm wondering for the thousandth time how he stays slim while slogging down full-fat lattes and eating fast-food burgers and fries, he calls my name.

"What's this?" he says in an unsteady voice.

I come out of the bathroom and drop my kit on the bed beside the suitcase before turning to see what Paolo's gotten into. I'm not secretive, so I can't guess what he's found. But when I see it, a lump rises in my throat. "It's nothing," I say, my tone unconvincing.

Paolo is holding up a shirt. On the surface, it's nothing special: long-sleeved, button-down, stonewash blue, more than a little wrinkled. But when I take it from his hand, it takes all my will not to snatch it and fling it back into the closet and slam the door. "It's nothing," I repeat, rolling it up like I never do with my other clothes, and putting it back on the top shelf where it came from.

Paolo cocks his head at me, messy curls falling over an eye. "Nothing, as in 'None of my business'?" he prompts, trying to be casual while radiating a mix of fear and jealousy. Though my heart is hammering in my chest, it's not about Paolo. And I'm not so far gone as to miss that he keeps his voice low and even, letting me know he's mostly scared. I'm not the jealous type, and Paolo knows I hate jealous lovers. But, like me, he left home in a bad way soon after coming out, so I understand his insecurity, even if I don't like it.

I sigh and sit on the edge of the bed. I'm waiting for Paolo to chill enough to tell me why he was going through my shit before I reassure him . . . and myself.

"Sorry," he mumbles, a little brother being scolded. But he comes and sits beside me, and he doesn't flinch or pull away when I put my hand on his thigh. "Really," he says, voice stronger. "I was just looking for the tank top I like, the white muscle one with the skinny straps." His pace picks up to a nervous babble. "I wanted to sneak it into your case before you came out of the bathroom so I could talk you into wearing it on the beach, even though I know you don't like it. And then I saw that blue shirt all balled up in the back of the top shelf . . ." When I squeeze his leg, he stops.

"I do hate that shirt," I say. Then to clarify: "The tank top." It doesn't look bad, but it's for others to see me in, not for me to enjoy wearing. I get enough looks at work. Sometimes I adore it, but this is supposed to be a vacation. All this thinking about the tank top makes me realize I'm avoiding the real subject. I need to play fair with Paolo.

I turn to look at him, but it takes a hand on his cheek to get him to face me. I want to say, "It's nothing," again, or "It doesn't matter," or "Don't worry about it." Instead, I kiss him, and he lets me. "It's what I was wearing when I left," I say, our mouths close, his breath warm and anxious on my face.

I'm long past crying, but seeing that shirt throws me back into the past like a fist to the chest. I keep it hidden so when I see it, it's on my own terms. Now, seemingly beyond my control, I'm remembering Ma and Ba's disapproving faces as they rattled off every offensive, automatic cliché they knew: I didn't know what I was saying, it was just a phase, they'd find me a nice girl. My mind is swimming through my senior year in high school, trying to believe my folks—though I never really did—miserably hiding who I was and what I wanted, drowning in therapy, guilt, and loneliness.

"You kept it, huh?" Paolo says softly, looking up at the shelf. He shrugs and his voice is more confident when he declares, "I didn't keep anything."

That's news to me. A lot of our knowledge of each other is shared in half-uttered descriptions and vague explanations. I know Paolo's parents were worse than mine. There had never been a question of throwing me out: I was the precious only child who just needed to get his head on straight, as it were. Paolo, by contrast, was one of three, the unimportant middle-born. They had flat-out told him he didn't deserve their love or protection. "Damned Catholics," I'd said when he told me his story after we fucked the first time. At least my folks were Buddhist. They'd kept religious condemnation out of it. From a distance of six years, I can see they mostly just wanted to be proud parents and grandparents, to boast to family back home and friends in town of their son the success. Instead, Paolo and I had both landed in San Francisco by our eighteenth birthdays, alone but hopeful. And that hope, with a little blood, sweat, and tears, had paid off—in all the ways that really mattered.

"Hey Trouble," I say with a grin. "Let's go feel each other up on Santa Monica beach."

"Let's," Paolo answers with a smile, his crooked front teeth more endearing than ever.

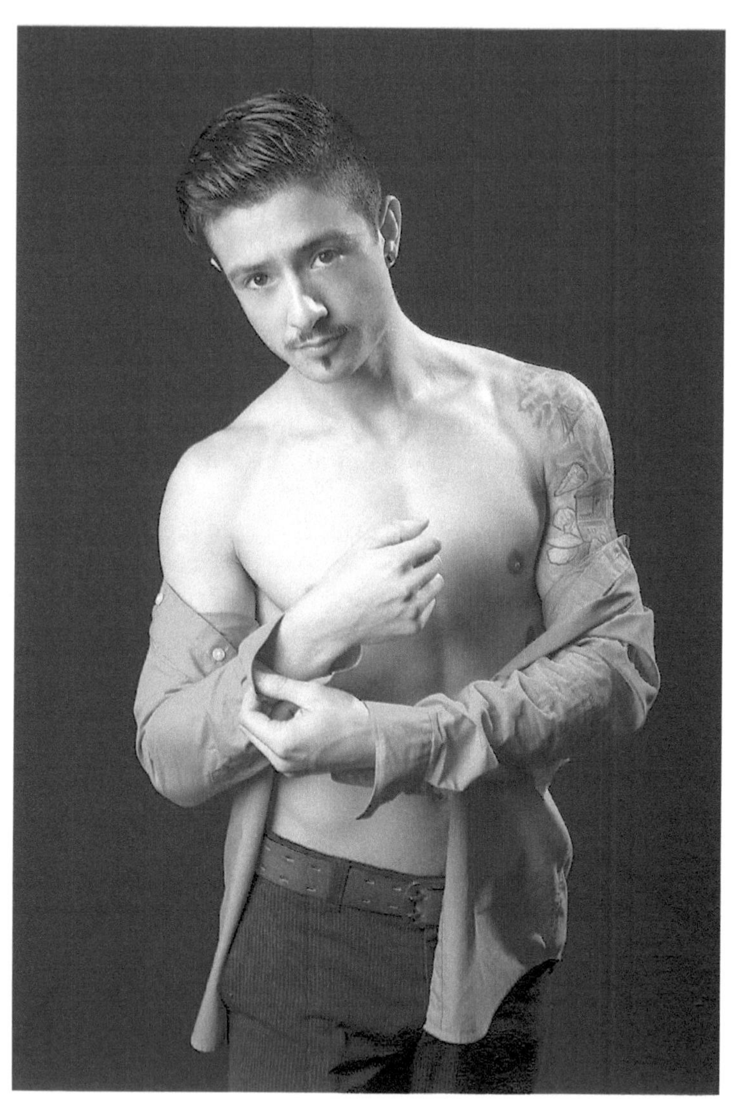

Ode to Projection

Trebor Healey

I asked him where he was from
Chula Vista was not what I'd hoped for
something Nahuatl, or Mixtec was always preferred

Well, his name was Jason Ramirez
and he spoke not a word of Spanish
And his smooth creamy coffee perfection was sullied
    by an artful urban tattoo
that dismissed his indigenous magic and sold him short
    as just another 21st century gay boy
which is, after all, what he is

Still, his hair is blue-blacker than any midnight north
    of Zacatecas
and the dark pools of his eyes suggest ancient rites
which we soon partake of
timeless as our youthful tangling
fresh green buds bursting out of soil black as the hair
    around his anus

Turns out he's got a master's degree in public health
and owns a condo
He reminds me I don't speak Gaelic
and that my eyes are grayer than they are blue

But still, he chose me
and still, I chose him
Our projections could not trump love

They are but clumsy keys after all
to open each other's doors
to find our way inside the ancient other

Where we share the primal truth of our flung seed
and all projections vanish in its blinding white light
that is the birth of stars
and laughter

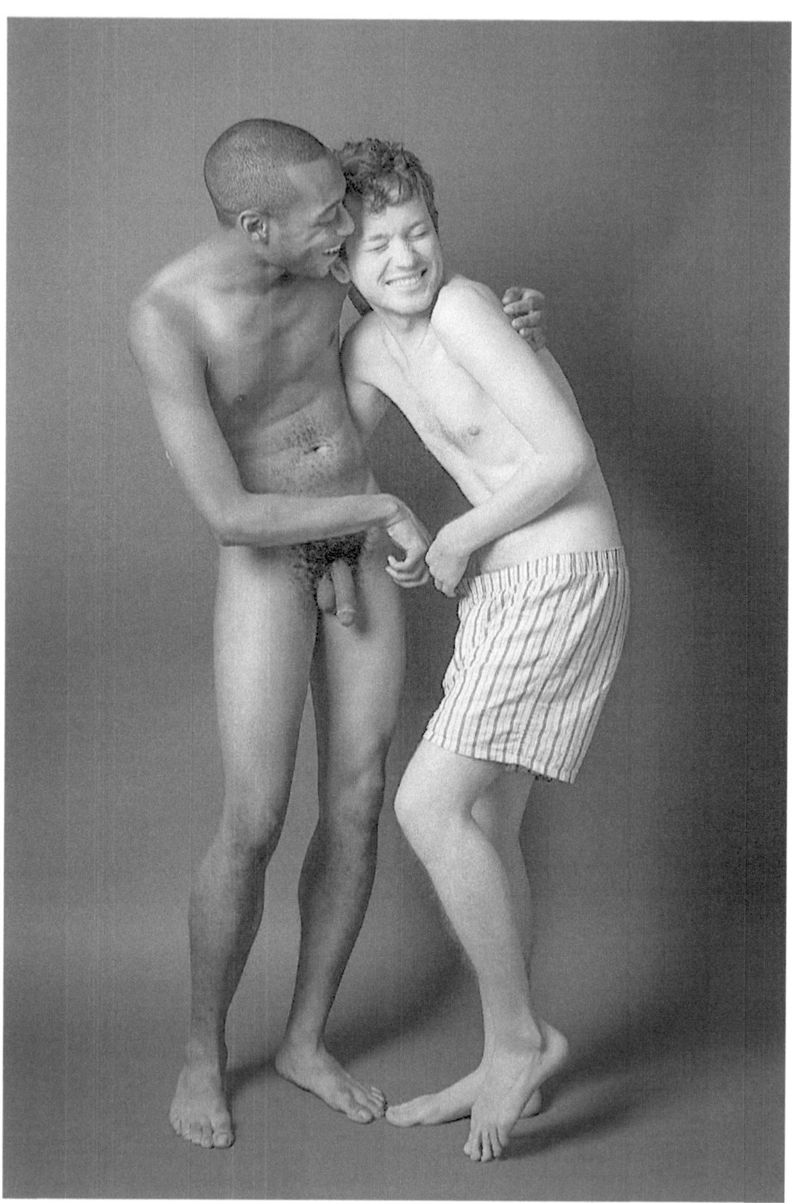

The Boxers

Jim Metzger

Cast

John: 20; undergraduate in English; grounded, kind.

Mikey: 20; undergraduate in Cellular Biology; flighty, quick-tempered, vulnerable.

Setting

Thursday, about 5:30 in the afternoon. The living room of a college apartment with couch, center; table and two chairs (unmatched), upstage left; side table stage right of couch. All strewn with clothes, dirty plates, books, journals, and coffee cups, both ceramic and take-outs from Starbucks and Peets. Stage left is the front door to the apartment; stage right is the door to the bedroom; upstage right is the door to the bathroom, ajar, showing a rack with a disheveled towel.

At Rise

Mikey enters stage left in jeans and a t-shirt, Levi jacket, and sneakers. He has on a full backpack and he carries a small gym bag. He drops the bag at the door and flings the backpack on the couch and begins rummaging through the clutter on the table.

John enters stage right, naked, rubbing his head with a towel. He crosses to Mikey, turns him around, kisses him, then lets his arms drape around him in a loose embrace.

JOHN: I talked to your mom today.

MIKEY: Where's my phone?

JOHN: *(Touches* MIKEY*'s lips with his fingertips, trying to get inside.)* We're meeting your sister for dinner at 7:30.

MIKEY: *(Squirming.)* Where's my phone?

JOHN: *(Lets* MIKEY *go and exits to bathroom to drop towel.)* You're back from school early.

MIKEY: *(Resumes his rummaging.)* I know. I left my phone. Have you been naked all day?

JOHN: *(Off.)* Uh-huh. Since morning. *(Re-enters.)* Are you going back to school, or do we get to finish what we started?

MIKEY: I was so late for class.

JOHN: You're always late.

MIKEY: You talked to my mom?

JOHN: She texted you over and over again, and when you didn't answer she sent me a 9-1-1. *(Pulls* MIKEY*'s phone from an item of clothing on the couch.* MIKEY *does not see this.)*

MIKEY: 9-1-1? Is she okay?

JOHN: *(Crosses to* MIKEY*, embraces him.)* Yes. She's fine. Everything's fine. *(Rubs* MIKEY*'s phone on his crotch before handing it off.)* Here's your dopa-phone, darling. Daddy gives you three minutes. *(*MIKEY *grabs phone.* JOHN *takes a novel from the side table, removes backpack from couch and sits.)* You're welcome.

MIKEY: *(Looking at phone.)* So my mom's okay? What was wrong? There're no text alerts or . . . Oh, here they are.

JOHN: It's your sister's birthday. Your mom needs you to buy a gift for Amy and deliver it on her behalf.

MIKEY: *(Reading screen.)* Hey, it's my sister's birthday! *(To* JOHN*.)* What did my mom want?

JOHN: *(Grabs phone, hides it under his leg.)* It's your sister's birthday.

MIKEY: I know that. Weren't you listening?

JOHN pulls MIKEY onto the couch and starts tickling him. Both start laughing. MIKEY tries to tickle JOHN back, but JOHN is clearly getting the better of him. MIKEY's laughter gets high, almost hysterical. He squirms and kicks. One of his shoes goes flying and the phone slides to the floor.

JOHN: Okay, calm down. Calm down, Mikey. . . . Good boy. Your mom wanted you to buy Amy a gift.

MIKEY: Oh my God, again? She's ridiculous. This happens every year.

JOHN: What, did Amy buy you a gift from your mom on your birthday?

MIKEY: Exactly. We both know she forgets, and then she calls us desperately at the last minute to fix it for her.

JOHN: Moms always have a reason. *(Pulls off* MIKEY*'s other shoe.)* Did you even know it was your sister's birthday?

MIKEY: Sure. Facebook just told me.

JOHN: So, no, you didn't.

MIKEY: Whatever. *(Rises.)* It doesn't matter. Amy and I are post-gifting.

JOHN: Post-gifting?

MIKEY: We need to be post-gifting. Millennials don't want gifts. Gifts are crap. "Happy Birthday! Here's some landfill!"

JOHN: Not if you put some thought into it.

MIKEY: Amy doesn't want anything. I don't want anything. We have everything we need. And if we don't, we just buy it. *(Grabs phone off floor.)*

JOHN: *(Rising.)* But you still didn't know it was her birthday. That's the problem.

MIKEY: Neither did my mom! Every year it's the same thing, and *I* have to buy a gift for Amy that *she* doesn't want. It's ridiculous and manipulative.

JOHN: There's a deeper reason.

MIKEY: My mom's a flake. Ever since Dad died, she's lost it.

JOHN: No, you're wrong. She does this on purpose, to remind you two to be a part of each other's lives. So when *she's* gone, you're still connected.

MIKEY: You're too optimistic.

JOHN: At least I'm trying. *(Sits on couch.)* It was fun shopping for Amy.

MIKEY: You bought her a gift?

JOHN: That's the whole point of this conversation.

MIKEY: Then *you* remember her when Mom dies.

JOHN pulls MIKEY to him, takes the phone from his hand and pulls MIKEY's tee-shirt off.

JOHN: It's okay to love people, Mikey. We don't all disappear like your dad.

MIKEY lies back, his head in JOHN's lap. JOHN strokes his hair.

MIKEY: Were you naked when you talked to my mom? Did you FaceTime?

JOHN: No. Of course not.

MIKEY: Why *are* you naked? Did you have someone over?

JOHN: Like I said, this is leftover from this morning. Someone stole my underwear. *(*JOHN *pokes* MIKEY *in the ribs. It tickles at first, then it hurts.)*

MIKEY: Ow. Are you calling me a thief?

JOHN: You do it every morning.

MIKEY: I like feeling close to you.

Silence for a moment.

JOHN: You wanna pick up where we left off?

MIKEY: *(Sits up, speaking to himself first, then to* JOHN*)* Oh! *That's* why I wanted to call. You won't believe who I saw today! P.M.S.!

JOHN: Professor Mumble Stud? Nice! I've missed the adventures of your irascibly hot lab TA. Where was he?

MIKEY: At the gym.

JOHN: Did it finally happen?

MIKEY: It did not happen.

JOHN: Did you at least say hi? Did he?

MIKEY: It's not that exciting.

JOHN: And that's why you wanted to call. To tell me nothing exciting happened.

MIKEY: What did you talk to my mom about?

JOHN: It *did* happen, or you wouldn't keep changing the subject. You fucked P.M.S.!

MIKEY: No. I'm just scattered, you know that. That's why I need you, a strong male role model to keep me in line. *(MIKEY begins playing with JOHN.)* Really, what did you tell her?

JOHN: Well, I told her everything that was going on with me, and you, and us. You really should make an effort to talk to her more. She's quite lovely, and lonely. You *will* call her tomorrow.

MIKEY: Maybe . . . What kind of crap did you get for my sister?

JOHN: A macramé hoodie scarf, in yellow.

MIKEY: That's actually perfect. So completely queer.

JOHN: Only if I knitted it myself.

MIKEY: *(Stands.)* Wait, you said you were naked all day.

JOHN: I'll say anything, Mr. Scientist, if it improves my chances of getting you naked.

MIKEY: I hate when you do that. I hate lies. The truth always works better with me.

JOHN: And I love to fuck. I love to fuck you. Whatever I say to make that happen is not a lie. It's simply a truth for fucking.

MIKEY: You and your post-modern relativism. My science hates your clever obfuscations. *(Sits, retrieves phone.)*

JOHN: I'll save you an inquisition. *(*JOHN *plucks the phone from* MIKEY*'s hand and rubs it sweetly over* MIKEY*'s body as he talks.)* Yes, I did get dressed today. Yes, your mom and I talked as I went around the corner to find a gift. And then, yes, as a thank you, she e-mailed me a Starbucks coupon, and I had a venti. And you know what that does to my shit.

MIKEY: You and your clean ass obsession.

JOHN: Exactly. I just got out of the shower when you got home.

MIKEY: *(Stands.)* That means *I* can fuck *you*! *(Removes belt.)*

JOHN: We've got about two hours till we meet your sister.

MIKEY: Oh, do we have to? I don't want to go.

JOHN: After all that talk about your mom? We're meeting up with Amy.

MIKEY: Who planned this, anyway?

JOHN: I did. By texting.

MIKEY: You're texting my sister now? We haven't been going out long enough for that.

JOHN: Dude, we live together.

MIKEY: Not officially.

JOHN: Oh, please! You, who wears my boxers almost every day. *(Removes* MIKEY*'s pants.)* Wait, those aren't my boxers.

MIKEY: I told you. P.M.S.

JOHN: You said you didn't fuck him.

MIKEY: I didn't.

JOHN: You only steal underwear from guys you fuck. How did this happen?

MIKEY: It's not very exciting.

JOHN: Something happened.

MIKEY: I guess I just got too worked up. I mean, come on, Professor Mumble Stud! He's like this mythic figure to me.

JOHN: He's definitely a mythic figure to *me*, and I've never even seen him.

MIKEY: You Googled him.

JOHN: That image was too grainy. He looked like a 3 AM tweaker on Scruff.

MIKEY: *(Modeling the boxers.)* He's so hot.

JOHN: Are they clean? *(Leans over and sniffs them.)*

MIKEY: Yes, shit-seeker, they're clean.

JOHN: I never would have thought he was a boxers man. Briefs, maybe, or commando. But boxers?

As the scene continues, JOHN and MIKEY get increasingly physical.

MIKEY: How would you know?

JOHN: The way you described him. I have imagination. I read. He's such a lost puppy, his tousled hair and stained shirts, the irritated smirking.

MIKEY: We were *way* off with him. We should start following him.

JOHN: You mean stalk him? Isn't stealing his boxers enough?

MIKEY: . . . So, anyways, for some reason he left his locker open when he went to the shower.

JOHN: Did you see . . . ?

MIKEY: No, total towelage, but there was definitely crotch landscape.

JOHN: So he *is* a stud! I knew it.

MIKEY: And then it got weird. I guess after months of drooling over him, I was overwhelmed, almost desperate. Before I knew it I was rifling through his gym bag.

JOHN: That is so wrong. I love it. Do you feel any moral ambiguity?

MIKEY: My snake brain does not care what my monkey mind is thinking.

JOHN: I love your snake—

Dopa-phone makes an incoming-text chime. JOHN and MIKEY freeze in the middle of their make-out. The phone repeats the chime. MIKEY breaks and picks up the phone.

MIKEY: *(Reading screen.)* "Gonna bring Stella to dinner. Hope you don't mind." Why is Amy texting me?

JOHN: I told you. She and I set up dinner plans.

MIKEY: Using my phone?

JOHN: Of course. I didn't have her number.

MIKEY: You posed as me?

JOHN: Sure.

MIKEY: How often do you do this?

JOHN: Every time you leave the room. I just wanna stroke your screen. I just want to be close to you. *(*MIKEY *glares at him.)* I'm joking.

MIKEY: Posing as me is not a joke.

JOHN: No, but it was efficient. It was the easiest way to help out you, your mom, and Amy.

MIKEY: By violating my privacy?

JOHN: Oh, fuck, boy. I knew this would happen.

Silence.

MIKEY: How do you know my passcode, anyway?

JOHN: I told you to change it.

MIKEY: Well, even if I didn't, that's not my fault. You were wrong to use it.

JOHN: Says the man who steals boxers from his lab TA.

MIKEY: That's not the same. You violated my trust.

JOHN: The only difference is that you *know* who violated *your* trust.

MIKEY: See? You admit it! I'm so pissed at you, John.

JOHN: Of course you are. You love being pissed, Mikey. You love making fights out of nothing.

MIKEY: And you love to diminish my feelings.

JOHN: I was simply doing you a favor, a favor you still haven't thanked me for.

MIKEY: Trust is bigger than whatever favor you thought you were doing.

JOHN: You know, I feel like there's some ambiguity in your charges. We're a couple. We help one another in a pinch. I'm pretty sure that's how it works.

MIKEY: *(Sits, looks at phone, hands it to* JOHN.*)* Here, text Amy back. Say, quote, "I'm bringing my asshole boyfriend. Hopefully he'll let me speak for myself."

JOHN: Look, I knew it wasn't the best decision at the time. It just seemed . . . quick. But I'm not apologizing until tomorrow, when we're both smart enough to hear one another. *(Hands phone back.)*

MIKEY: Thank you.

JOHN: *Now* you thank me. Well, I may as well get dressed. No sex for Daddy. Mind if I rifle through your bag, since that's supposedly not morally problematic?

MIKEY: Stop vilifying me.

JOHN: I'm not. I *love* my five fingered brief-thief. It's your villainy that brought us together. Where's my underwear?

MIKEY: It's not there.

JOHN: What? *(Silence.)* Those are my favorite pair.

MIKEY: I know.

JOHN: Those were *the* pair.

MIKEY: I know.

JOHN: What were you thinking?

MIKEY: I wasn't. I was flustered. I've never taken boxers from someone I haven't slept with, so I figured I had to leave a pair, so that P.M.S. would know another man was wearing his. A post-hetero protest, like you talk about, right?

JOHN: A post-hetero protest is telling a straight boy he's a hottie without shame. Trading away our special pair of underwear to P.M.S. was just the wrong choice. You need to get them back.

MIKEY: What? How?

JOHN: You know where his office is. You were there almost every day last year.

MIKEY: I can't do that. How about I just forgive you for using my phone.

JOHN: You're the one who said those issues are not the same.

MIKEY: Yes, but I was wrong. In the same way I said using my phone was a denial of my privacy, stealing P.M.S.'s underwear is, like, a symbolic denial of his.

JOHN: You're gonna talk symbols with an English major? You're gonna lose. I could easily claim that the underwear you traded away was, perhaps, *the* greatest symbol of our relationship. *(Silence.)* That it was *the* underwear you stole from me after our first hook up. *(Silence.)* That because of that little thievery, I tracked you down, knocked on your door, and when you opened it, and I saw you standing there, still wearing my boxers two days later, I instantly fell in love with you.

MIKEY: I know.

JOHN: You were *so* cute.

MIKEY: I know. Oh God. How pissed are you? You're *so* pissed, aren't you? Is this break-up-able?

JOHN: No. No drama. If our relationship is based on symbolic underwear, we're doomed. I just want them back.

MIKEY: I can't get them back.

JOHN: I want them back.

MIKEY: Wouldn't it make more sense for you to get them? I mean, he doesn't know you, so it wouldn't be embarrassing.

JOHN: Why would he ever admit anything about stolen underwear to some random stranger who happens to drop by his office? How would I even know where his office is? It makes no sense.

MIKEY: But it's so embarrassing.

JOHN: *(Laughs.)* Well, no pressure, post-hetero—even if, perhaps, doing it *just might be* the greatest symbol of our relationship.

MIKEY: Think of my reputation in the department.

JOHN: He won't tell anyone. It's too weird.

MIKEY: Oh my God.

JOHN: Weren't you muttering about needing an assertive role model to help keep you in line, boy?

MIKEY: I have to do this?

JOHN: You want them back, too, don't you?

MIKEY grimaces, then nods.

JOHN: We both want them back. But you're a brave little boy, Mikey. *(He gives him a tickle.)* You can do it.

They laugh softly, exchanging tickles that turn into caresses. The dopa-phone chimes and buzzes. They ignore it.

CURTAIN

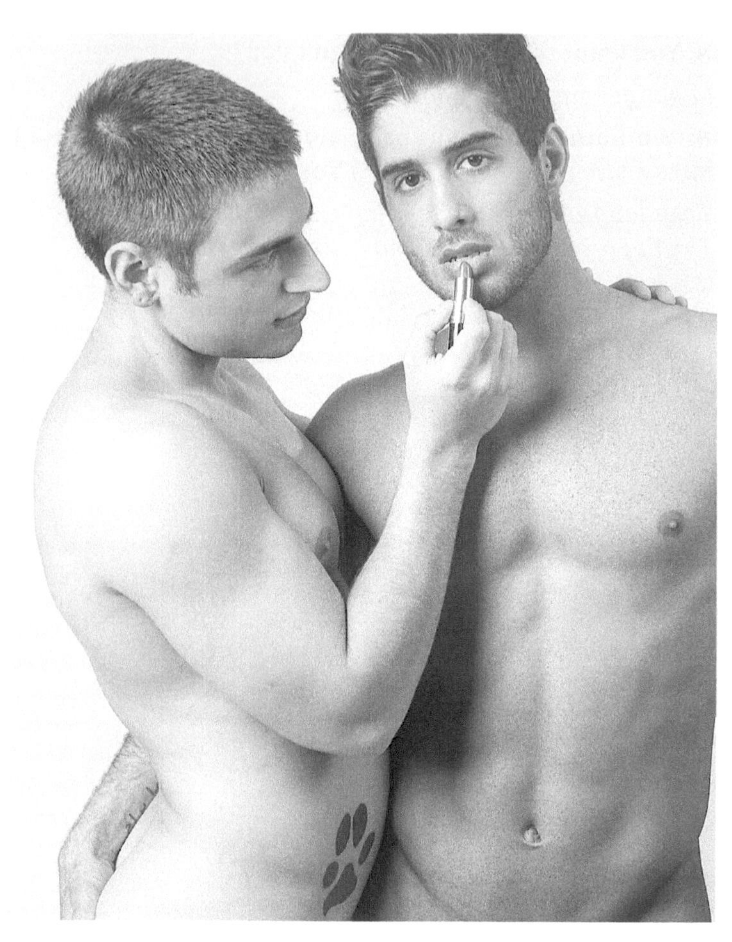

Adonis
Rob Rosen

I'd had one too many at the bar. Actually, to be exact, I had three too many. Well, maybe four. It had been a particularly bad day at work. I'd never been to this place before, but it was the closest gay dive I could find. So when I finally made it off the stool—no easy feat, mind you—and headed for the bathroom, it was no wonder that I accidentally zigged when I should've zagged, winding up not in said bathroom but in, it appeared, a dressing room.

I squinted into the light of the place, which was somewhat spinning at the time like a tilt-a-whirl. I took a deep breath and promptly coughed, the aroma of powder and hairspray and any number of unidentifiable scents promptly invading my sinus cavity. A woman sat at a vanity table applying lipstick to her rather full lips. "Oh," I managed. The word, though a mere two letters, was slurred and drawn out. "Sorry, ma'am."

She laughed, the sound deep and rumbling like the ocean during a storm, pitching me to and then fro. "Girl, you don't look so good," she said as she stood up—um, towered up, actually.

"Damn," I said. "They sure do grow them big in your parts."

She raised an eyebrow. "If you only knew."

But I didn't know. I didn't know where I was or what she was talking about. In fact, if you would have asked me my name right about then, I probably would have gotten it wrong. Oh, and it's David, by the way. Thank you for asking.

"Ma'am, there a bathroom around here?"

She pointed behind her. "You gonna throw up in there, sweetie? Because I'll hand you a mop as well."

I thought about it for a second. So did my belly, which trembled and shook, but then thankfully settled down some. "Nope. Just pee."

"You need any help?" She grinned mischievously.

Again, I thought about it for a second. I didn't exactly like the idea of a woman helping me go the bathroom, and so I replied, "Nah, I'm good." Which was a matter of debate.

She shrugged. Her hair teetered. I teetered in solidarity. She held my hand and led me to her private can. She stood behind me as I dropped my pants. I pressed my hand against the wall for support, then let out a sigh and a splashing yellow stream. "*Aaah.*"

"Better, sweetie?"

Again, I gave it a second. "Think you can call me a cab?"

Her laugh returned, rumbling through me like a runaway locomotive. "You look more like a cub than a cab, but, sure, no problem."

Everything sort of got fuzzy after that. Or, um, fuzzier. Actually, I don't quite remember much after that point. I recall the cold tile of the dressing room bathroom, the stinking smell of the cab the lady helped me into, and me hitting my bed like a ton of bricks. Then everything went dim, dimmer, and ultimately black. When I awoke some indeterminable amount of time later, my head felt like a log had been split over it. "Ouch," I said with a wince, grabbing for my noggin as I glanced groggily at the clock on the side table. It was just after eleven in the morning on Sunday. I had no intention of moving off my bed for fear that my head would roll right off my neck. "Ouch," I repeated. Talk about your gross understatements.

And then, as if things weren't bad enough, there came a loud *knock! knock!* on my front door. "You've got to be kidding me." I ignored it. I wasn't expecting anybody, was I? I racked my brain, except that my brain had up and quit on me. Or maybe it had travelled south and was tending to my abused liver. Again I heard the knocking, which was louder this time and echoing in my brain-free head. "Please stop," I whined. "Please." But the knocker didn't hear me or, if they did, was summarily ignoring my plea.

I gave up and rolled out of bed, landing on the floor with a loud *kerthump.* I was still wearing my clothes from the night before. They'd bunched up in all the wrong places and smelled a hell of a lot worse than when I'd left for the bar. The knocking continued; the pounding in my head did the same. "I'm coming!" I shouted, which hurt like a mother-fucker. "Mother fucker!" I aptly added.

I flung the door open. "What the—" I stared at the Adonis standing before me "—fuck." Tall, dark and handsome didn't even begin to cover it. His smile was perfect, tan perfect, eyes perfect, shoulders and waist—well, you get the drift. If this was the welcome wagon, then he was more than welcome. Knock all the fuck you want. "Can I help you?" *Wash your hair, walk your dog, paint your house? Just ask,* I thought to myself.

"David?"

I scratched my head. "Do I know you?" *Oh to be so lucky.*

He grinned. Somewhere there was an orthodontist with a rather large trophy case. "We've met."

"Really?" Stood to reason I'd remember. I willed my brain back to its home base. It ignored my request. Stupid brain. "Recently?"

He nodded. "Very." He handed me my wallet. I automatically reached for the back of my jeans. My wallet wasn't there. Hence the fact that he had it. Made sense. Heck, he could keep it so long as he continued standing there with it. Actually, I wondered if he would've minded if I got my camera and took a picture of him with it. Or just him. For posterity's sake. I started to ask when he held his free hand out and said, "I'm Chuck."

I grabbed his hand, a spark of electricity riding down my spine before exploding in my crotch. There was an instant connection, a tethering of sorts, like one of us had docked in the other's port. "Of course you are." I coughed. "I mean, nice to meet you." I pocketed my wallet. "And, uh, thanks. How come you have it and I don't?"

The grin rose northward on his handsome, stubbled face. "You lost it at the bar last night."

Ah, now that made sense. "Did you happen to find my brain, too?"

He laughed. It sounded strangely familiar, rumbling like an earthquake. And damn if my earth wasn't quaking. "I think you might've had a tad too much to drink last night."

"Was there any vodka left on the shelf?"

He suddenly stared very intently at me. I fixed my hair in response and wiped my lips and rubbed the sleep from my eyes. Why was he staring? Why was I staring? Why was no one talking? *Talk! Say something!* "Um, right," he said. "Well, I guess I should go then."

"No!" I shouted. He jumped. "I mean, no, don't go. Let me at least offer you a cup of coffee." *Or a pot of it. Hell, take the whole Keurig.*

"You really don't remember meeting me?" he asked.

I grinned. Even that hurt. "Trust me, if I did, I'd know it." I blushed. That hurt as well. "Please, come in. Just a cup. I think—scratch that, *I know*—I could use one."

Again he stared at me. Clearly, he was weighing his options. I wondered why. Did I look a fright? Damn if I didn't feel like one. Still, his lustrous smile quickly returned. "You got any cake to go with that coffee?"

My stomach gurgled. Suddenly, I was starving. "German chocolate okay?"

"You had me at chocolate."

And he had me at *knock! knock!* "Please, come in." Or just come. Your choice. I have plenty of towels to help with the cleanup.

I prayed I was just thinking these thoughts instead of saying them, but given my current state of mind, I wasn't laying any bets. In any case, he walked in and I followed close behind, staring longingly down at his denim-encased ass as it swayed from side to side.

He sat in my dining room. I passed a painting on the wall and caught my reflection in the glass. I fought back a gasp. No wonder he was staring at me funny. I looked like a makeover's "Before" picture. In fact, I looked like before the "Before."

"I'll start the coffee, Chuck," I said, handing him the half-uneaten cake along with a fork, forgetting to offer a plate or a napkin. He stared from said cake to me and back again. He grinned. I grinned in return. "And while it's brewing, I think I might, you know, straighten up a bit." *And look for my brain and perhaps a comb. Or a rake, considering the state of my hair.*

"You look fine."

Pot. Kettle. Black. "It'll only take me a moment." *God willing.*

And so I ran from the dining room and into my bathroom, shucking my stinking jeans, T-shirt, and socks as I simultaneously combed my hair, brushed my teeth, and scrubbed my face. FYI, it's nearly impossible to shuck your clothes as you comb, brush, and scrub, but when there's an Adonis eating German chocolate cake in your dining room, sans plate and napkin, you manage. Not well, mind you, but you manage just the same.

Naked and covered in soap, suds, and toothpaste, there came a new knocking, this time my bathroom door. "Just a minute," I grunted.

"Are you okay?"

I stared at myself in the mirror. I was clearly not okay. "I'm fine."

"You don't sound fine."

I nodded. He had me there. I sighed. "I'm fine." Or perhaps I will be in a day or so. Give or take. Mostly give.

He knocked again. "I'm coming in."

He opened the door and knocked me over. I sat sprawled on the floor, naked and covered in soap, suds, and toothpaste, my clothes in a heap behind me. "Yeah," he said, suppressing a laugh. "Right as rain."

I stared up as he stared down. "Cake any good?"

He shrugged. "Not bad." He crouched down and stroked my balls with the undersides of his fingertips. I squirmed in delight. "You sure you don't need any help?"

I forced a smile. Actually, nix that; I beamed with joy. Or at least joy*ish*, given my present state, which was tenuous at best. "Help," I replied, all of a sudden nearly breathless.

"Gladly," he replied, his fingers were replaced by his mouth and tongue, both of which worked wonders, causing my prick to rise from horizontal to stiff and mostly vertical in about two seconds flat.

"You're very good at helping," I couldn't help but say.

My cock came out of his mouth in an audible *pop*. "Saint Chuck, at your service."

I nodded. "And a disciple should be able to return the favor."

"Sounds biblical."

I laughed. "Doubtful." I pointed at his state of dress, which was not the one I preferred. "In any case . . ."

He got the hint and hopped back up. I in turn grabbed my wrinkled shirt and quickly wiped away the soap, suds, and toothpaste, then propped my head on my bunched up jeans and gratefully watched as he began to undress. First came his sneakers, then his socks, revealing high arches and massive feet. I gulped at the implication. Up and off came his T-shirt, his chest just as massive, his belly a six pack with a seemingly extra set of cans, all of it smooth, all of it etched to perfection. *Adonis? Please, Mary. Adonis should be so lucky.*

"You like?" he asked.

Again, I nodded. "Better than German chocolate cake."

"First time I've ever heard it said quite that way, but thanks."

"You're welcome," I replied. "And please continue." *And hurry!*

He grinned, and the light in the room seemed to amp up a few hundred watts. His belt got unbuckled next, jeans unbuttoned and unzipped, the sound like a swarm of horny bees zooming around my head. Down came the denim and out shot his prick. My newfound friend, it seemed, went commando. Blessed Saint Chuck!

He was naked in two seconds. I was sucking his swollen prick in even less. It seems that blowing someone who's hung is the perfect cure for a hangover. I'd have to remember that the next time I went out drinking. Or better still, revel in the revelation now. And so I sucked and slurped with wild abandon as I tugged his balls, which hung like boulders from his crotch, with one hand and stroked my own billy club with the other. *I've heard of perfect strangers before,* I thought, *but this gives the term a whole new meaning.*

I retracted his cock from my mouth. "You ever wonder what it would be like to get fucked in a stranger's bathroom?"

He laughed and scratched his chin and squinted up at the ceiling. "Now that you mention it, no. No, I hadn't ever wondered that." He gazed back down at me. "Before now, that is. Now it's all I can think about."

I jumped up to retrieve a rubber and some lube, so as to put the thought into the realm of actuality, but then stopped, sighed at the heady aroma of him, and mashed my lips into his. Our mouths joined as one, our tongues doing an oral tango above as our cocks mamboed below. I moaned as he pulled me in tight, the sound crescendoing as he tweaked and tugged on my nipples.

Eventually, I said, "I should go now."

"Really?"

I went back to kissing him. The lube and the rubber could wait.

Ten minutes later, however, my prick was sheathed and he was bent over the sink, staring at me from the reflection in the mirror, his stunning ass jutting out, his pink, crinkled hole winking my way. This being Sunday, I knelt down and prayed at his alter, worshiping his holy trinity: ass and hole and hovering prick. My tithing was a tongue buried deep inside his chute, and far more than the commanded ten percent.

I stood again and slapped my prick against his puckered portal. I doused them both with ample quantities of lube and then teased my wide, helmeted head inside. He sucked in his breath, his ring tightening around my tingling cock, his back arching. Once he relaxed, I slid on home, Fourth of July fireworks bursting forth behind my fluttering eyelids.

"*Fuuuck,*" he exhaled.

"Yeah," I replied. "I'm getting to that."

I popped my tool out again. It stood at rapt attention, aiming dead ahead. In I shoved, filling him to the brim as he let out a long, low moan. Again it came out, my cock on fire, his ass practically begging for more. And so more is what I gave him, the cub fucking the god. I gazed at the odd yet hot pairing of us in the mirror as I pumped in and out, in and out, the tiled bathroom walls echoing our moans and groans and guttural grunts.

"Wait, wait," he soon panted. "Lay down, flat on your back. I want to watch you come. I want you to watch me come."

I readily agreed. "Sounds like a plan."

We wound up with me back on the bathroom floor and him hovering just above my mast of a cock before he sat and ground his rump into my crotch. I stared at him as his boner bounced up and down while his ass did the same and my cock appeared and disappeared in rapid succession. It was like fucking a giant. Odd, like I said, yet hot. Scorching actually. And to think an hour earlier I had been in hangover hell; now I was in blissed-out heaven. Seriously, I must've saved a boatload of kittens in a previous life to deserve such joyous karma. I grabbed his pole of a prick and jacked him as he rode me like a bucking, fucking bronco. *Yeehaw!* By then I was close. I mean really, you try fucking an Adonis and see if you don't come in about two minutes.

And then, as the saying goes, into each life a little rain must fall. Except this was a torrential downpour. Even Noah would've been discouraged.

See, Chuck stared down at me, eyes boring home, and as he rode me for dear life, he said, "Better, sweetie?"

I froze, mid-pump. "Huh?"

"From your hangover," he said. "Because you look a lot fucking better now."

"Sweetie," I coughed out.

He tilted his head as his hole engulfed my prick. "Okay. Because you look a lot fucking better now, *sweetie*."

And the memories came flooding back, like a dam had suddenly burst. *Damn dam*. "I lost my wallet last night in the bar."

He nodded. "I thought we covered that." He squinted down at me. "You okay?"

"I lost it in a dressing room." I paused. "In *your* dressing room." Again I paused. "That wasn't a woman I was talking to last night, that was . . ."

He grinned. "Lucy Taintia, at your service, sweetie."

I coughed. I was fucking a drag queen. I didn't know how to feel about the fact. I mean, Adonis didn't earn his living dressing up as a woman and lip-synching to Cher, did he? Was I simply being misogynistic? Did the term even apply here, considering he wasn't even a woman? My head suddenly hurt again, and my heart didn't feel too much better. And, oddly enough, my cock started withering on the proverbial vine.

"Um," I managed.

He seemed to realize my dilemma and eased himself off, rolling away from my prick before landing on his knees by my side. "You don't like it that I'm a drag queen?"

My chest tightened. "Part time, right? I mean, you're a mechanic during the day, a brick layer, a defensive lineman?"

He shook his head. "An offensive one-liner man, maybe, but, no, David, I make a decent living as a drag queen. Plus, I love what I do." He sighed. "Houston, do we have a problem here?"

"But look at you." I pointed at the glorious him there was to look at. Which was substantial. "You don't look like a drag queen."

"Not now, no. But give me a pound of concealer and a wig the size of Cleveland, and just watch me go."

I winced at the thought. Suddenly, I understood why people got so mad at the whole bait-and-switch scheme. I'd been baited and he'd done the switching—into a girdle. *Fuck, fuck, fuck.* "I, um . . . it's just . . . you know . . . "

His smile vanished altogether. "No, David, I don't know." He stood up. "I like what I do. And I thought I liked you. I even thought you liked me. That's what it felt like." He pointed to his stunning ass. "Everywhere, I might add."

Now here's the sad truth: I did like him. I didn't know him, clearly, and I still liked him. It's as if we had an instant bond. Still, I couldn't move beyond the fact that he dressed up in, well, dresses for a living. I was brought up in a macho household with three brothers. The two worlds were too incongruent. Besides, what would my friends say? What would my family say? What would my dry cleaner say when she found lipstick on my shirts? I mean, she just got used to the whole gay thing; how could I suddenly confuse her like this? How could I confuse myself like this?

"I should go," he said, once the pause in the conversation grew so large that you could drive a Mack Truck through it.

Oh, how I hated to say it, but I still did. "Yeah, that might be best."

And that's how I ended up alone in my bathroom, on my back, naked, and, once again, hung-over. Meaning, I might've saved a boatload of kittens, but somehow they still all drowned. Not a pretty picture, but trust me, nothing about this was pretty. Well, Chuck was pretty, sure, but my feelings toward Lucy, um, not so much. And, yes, I realized they were both the same person, but I couldn't get beyond the yin to his yang—even though he had one mighty fine yang.

I went back to bed. I went back to sleep. Or at least tried to. Suffice it to say, I failed, miserably. I just couldn't stop thinking about Chuck. Then again, I couldn't stop thinking about Lucy either. And therein lay my problem. That is to say, I could lay one, but not the other.

A day went by, two, a week. I couldn't get Chuck out of my head—not the big one or the little one. I had been wrong. Deep down, I knew it. But what was I to do? He probably hated me. Heck, I hated me.

So I went back to the bar, avoiding the vodka this time. I headed to the back, to the show. I stopped in my tracks. Lucy Taintia was on the stage. She wasn't lip-synching to Cher; she was cracking jokes. The audience was in hysterics. Soon enough, so was I, laughing at the man of my dreams, even though I never dreamed he'd be in a maternity muumuu.

Toward the end of his act, he spotted me in the back of the crowd. His face went from a smile to a frown and back to a smile again. Probably nobody noticed. Nobody, that is, but me.

He left the stage. I knew where he went. And so I looped around the bar and headed for the dressing room, returning to the scene of the crime.

"You're back," he said, the wig now gone, muumuu as well. "What did you lose this time?"

I grinned, trying to appear cute. "My mind?"

He smiled in reply. "Duh."

I moved in closer. "Look, I'm sorry."

"For?"

"For being a jerk."

His smile grew wider. "And?"

"Not seeing past the surface of things."

He nodded. "That's a good one. And?"

I snapped my fingers. "Not making you come!"

"Ding, ding, ding," he chimed, at last closing the gap between us. "I forgive you, provided that—" He paused.

"Provided that I make you come?"

"See, I knew you were smart, despite insulting a drag queen. That's what happened at Stonewall, and just look at all the shit that went down there." He turned and locked the dressing room door. "And speaking of going down."

I nodded and started to fall to my knees, but realized one more thing I needed to do. And so I grabbed his lipstick and smeared it across my lips. It smelled odd beneath my nose, waxy, and made my lips feel heavy. "A peace offering, if you will." I then spread the red across his mouth. The color suited him.

He grabbed his crotch. "Yeah, I have your peace offering right here." He laughed. "Sweetie."

Oh how joyful that word sounded. In fact, it sounded about how I felt. And so I laughed and fell to my knees and awaited my prize for at last realizing just how big an idiot I had been. I had judged a book by its nylon-encased cover. It was a mistake I'd never make again.

He dropped his panties—a rather fetching, pink lacy pair—to the floor and untucked his mammoth prick.

"God, that looks painful," I couldn't help but say as I watched it untangle before arcing up and out.

"But just look how happy it is when it gets to come out and play."

"Emphasis on the come part."

He nodded and slapped his hefty tool against my cheek. "Obviously."

I swallowed it, the lipstick smearing down his shaft, his neatly trimmed pubes now tinged with magenta. The makeup was raspberry flavored. His dick tasted like a Popsicle. And so I sucked it with glee as I stared up at him and he stared down at me, stroking my hair all the while.

I almost missed out on this. On him. On us. Almost, but not quite. *Thank you, God.*

"Can two play at this game?" he soon rasped.

His prick popped out of my mouth. "I thought two were." Still, I got his drift, and unleashed my beast and lay on the floor. We were in a perfect sixty-nine not two seconds later. I inhaled his scent: musk and sweat and sex, with perhaps a bit of perfume that wafted down from parts unknown.

He pulled off me soon and panted, "Close."

"Closer," I replied. My hand replaced my mouth, furiously jacking his prick, watching, waiting for the inevitable.

He stroked in sync with me, his eyes on the prize, seemingly eager for the spectacle. As to that, I didn't disappoint.

I moaned loudly as I came, jizz erupting like Vesuvius, molten-hot spunk shooting up before raining down in big, white globs that splattered my jeans and the floor. I bucked my dick into his still beating fist, my balls unleashing a week's worth of juice.

Chuck came right along with me, a rumble of a groan travelling down his body and through my wrist. His cock grew even thicker as he shot, come bubbling from his slit before cascading over the girthy sides. My hand was sticky with it, the aroma both sweet and sour, intoxicating, just like him.

When at last we were done and had caught our breaths, we scooted around and swapped some heavy spit, lipstick everywhere, all over our mouths and chins. I laughed when I finally broke away and was able to get a good look at him.

"Not to rain on our little pride parade," he said, "but I'm on again in ten minutes."

I frowned, good-naturedly, and squeezed his withering cock. "What a drag."

"Amen, sweetie," he whispered into my ear as he hugged me good and tight. "Amen to that."

Ted's Pantyhose

Miles Griffis

Turn the stick and paint your lips quite red
Pull on those pantyhose and look me in the eye
And uh, kiss me before I throw ya on the bed

Boogey that booty, that's right that's what I said
How 'bout you uh, put a hand on my thigh
Turn the stick and paint your lips quite red

Don't be shy now, come on now you're drop dead
So how 'bout you uh, bite off my bow tie
And uh, lick me before I throw ya on the bed

Get a little lower and uh, go right ahead
How 'bout we get real steamy like July
Turn the stick and paint your lips quite red

Let's go at it like stallions till we're bred
Let's go at it till we're both bone dry
And uh, kiss me before I throw ya on the bed

I like you in all this pretty stuff Ted
You look real dainty for a big ripped guy
Turn the stick and paint your lips quite red
And uh, kiss me before I throw ya on the bed

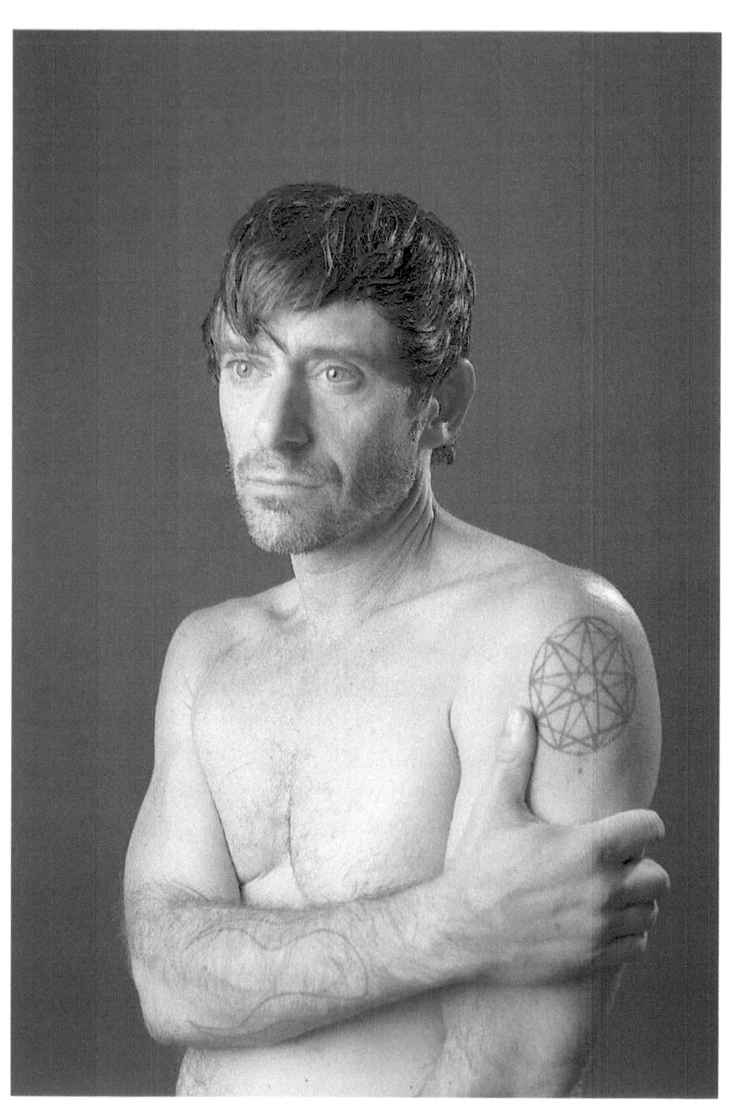

Summer: A History
Erik Schuckers

We live with a mouse-furred box fan in three small rooms and an attic on the South Side, around the corner from a Spanish restaurant, a tattoo parlor, and the gay bookstore.

The chlorine stench of old paella rises from a dumpster. Swaths of asphalt split beneath our neighbors' lawn chairs, markers for their battered, truant Buicks. The summer heat is personal. It thickens in our lungs as we haul bags of humid clothes to the laundromat. It pushes through the car vents; vinyl and plastic sear our fingerprints. Our shadows waver and flee.

We're cracking up.

You work nights at Lucky's. You've scored the Sunday crowds, drinking off the start of another week, and picked up Wednesdays' hardcore revelers halfway to release. Most of the boys are spectacularly thin: ragged, greasy strays right off the Greyhound.

My type, not yours.

Years of careful workouts have recast you from a slack-haired college kid not quite too shy to kiss to a toned ex-frat boy. From the planes of your smooth chest to your tattoos and roughened cheeks, you've built yourself into a cum pony.

You dance on the bar, your thighs wreathed in bills and cigarette smoke.

*

Things your parents write: *He was an Eagle Scout. He loved waterskiing and downhill skiing, music and books. He loved animals, especially his dogs.*

*

You cup Taz's gray muzzle to calm him as we talk treatments, yours and his. He's gone blind. You bear him up and down the stairs, swab his urine from the floors.

After eighteen years, we live ten minutes from our old place, from each other. Through Facebook, you invite me to dinner. At Thai Spoon, you give me the diagnosis.

You're not working. Disability helps, and your parents.

They've commissioned a new house in which to entertain. I haven't seen it. I only know the one your mother chased you out of, mad with disinfectant and rubber gloves, while I drove getaway. Now they help pick up the bills for Houston, the flights and hotel rooms, nutritionists and therapies.

You've grown conservative. Sometimes when we meet, you bitch about welfare and affordable care. We argue over curry shrimp and sesame chicken, through omelets and pancakes and afternoon salads, all surrendered greens and puckered tomatoes.

When I change the subject your smile is a sliver of moon on our first ripped mattress.

I walk you home when you're unsteady: we move like old soldiers. You still smoke, the flick of your lighter a small shrug. The metaphors are dollar bills accumulating against your skin. I slip them one by one.

It does not occur to me that you might be frightened.

*

You dance on the bar, deft among bottles of Rolling Rock and anxious hands. We've ruled against monogamy: look at the Romantics or Bloomsbury, the Beats, The Factory.

But you're not Candy Darling, and I'm not Gregory Corso, and Duncan Grant did not cruise Liberty at 3 am, high on whippits and arcade three-ways with Dior counter clerks and barbacks.

I watch *gialli*. I listen to Marianne Faithfull. Finally, in an airless dark that wraps the city like steaming muslin, comes the kind of conversation that ends in apologies at dawn, knot-gut nausea.

You take the attic. Sensible people, ones with money, would move out, cut losses, nurse wounds. We own no Fiestaware, no joint investment. Instead, we've got student loans, too many jobs, a car that doesn't start in winter, families remote or unforgiving.

And so we share a mouse-furred box fan, three small rooms, and an attic.

*

Things your parents write: *He was a member of the Pennsylvania Bible Teaching Fellowship and loved the Lord.*

*

We dismantle your dungeon.

We take down the chains that hold your sling, deconstruct St. Andrew's Cross. Your basement's musty, nostalgic with damp and leather and semen, sweat-socks and pot. A captain's daughter sits atop a cardboard box of textbooks.

We talk about college, about Scott, in Massachusetts and the academic life, and Danny, the beautiful blond diver who was not quite our lover nor our younger brother. We measure the perils of old houses we can't keep up, middle-aged bodies we can't not.

You talk about the guys you meet online, the dark downstairs at Donny's, the piss troughs and the awkward conversations in your lounge, with hardwood floors that need refinishing and an honest-to-God antimacassar on the sofa.

I talk about gardens and contractors, writing, poems playing coy, refusing to commit, slipping into notebooks undone, unlined. Not because my thoughts are fine or interesting. Because I am not having sex, and most of the people we could gossip about are dead, or in London.

We do not talk about HIV, the complications for your chemo. We do not talk about your status, or mine, the ground between them. We do not talk about that summer.

*

Very early one morning, I get up to vomit through the night's cheap Zinfandel. You stand vacant at the mirror, trick tucked in the attic. I imagine my arrival might coax you back to him, but you wait while I heave my way toward grim sobriety.

"He wants me to pee in his mouth. Do you think that's weird?"

I curl my entire body around the porcelain toilet base, the one cool surface in the whole apartment.

A few days later, I come home from work. You slump, drooling, on the toilet, jeans around your ankles, a crumpled paper bag between your right foot and the wall. Your eyes are closed. You grin, rock gently back and forth.

The apartment is silent.

I reach under your arms and pull you to your feet. You stand, swaying, while I zip up your fly. I walk you to our cast-off couch and ease you into the nubby fabric. I gather up the bag and empty the small brown bottle into the sink. A blast of cold water dilutes the smell.

*

Your father sends an email from your Facebook account: *He has days or a week. Pray for him*. He does not answer my messages. He does not write again.

*

Before we meet, your parents send you to counseling to unlearn yourself. It doesn't take. Later, money and your need for affection draw curtains through which you are sometimes glimpsed. You go underground, keep your secrets. From them, from me.

Mutual acquaintances, Christians vetted by your parents but treacherously kind, give me the name of your hospice.

I email Scott, married at last to Shinji, and Danny, adopting another child with his husband. Not Brad, shot dead in Oaxaca, who kissed me one night when we argued, or Timmy, gone eight years in October, those Halloweens at Resaca Place, the crushed red velvet sofa, the perilous staircase, vanished.

I visit Lucky's. The same songs on the jukebox downstairs: someone's playing "Edge of Seventeen." The guitar riff ripples the watered-down drafts. Upstairs, skinny boys dance at three corners of the bar, and Stevie's voice floats up to join the thump and grind.

Scott and Danny email me. Mike sends a confession, his crush on you: that night at The Eagle, you remember? "Edge of Seventeen" plays on WDVE as I drive home, your hospital address printed from MapQuest, folded in the glove compartment. I stall for time, too polite to make a scene. I remember your mother's face at the window as we drove away. What's my claim, after all, and after all this time?

I'm rich with reasons, rolling in them.

*

While you sleep on the couch, I walk into the sweltering afternoon to St. Elmo's. The bookstore does good business in New Age sidelines; it smells of incense and oiled wood. I linger in the air conditioning. A retro clone—wide black mustache, close-cropped hair, tight jeans—stands at the register.

He smiles as I leave, nothing claimed but cool air and a free *City Paper*.

A few blocks down, Tom's Diner is quiet. I revel in the chill of the cracked vinyl against my back, the smooth Formica beneath my palm. I order iced tea, and the waitress, archetype of diner waitresses, Queen Mother of the Brassy Beehive, clicks her pen in time with her gum as she walks away.

The paper's got a thermometer on the cover, teasing a story about the weather, unyielding and witless. I page through the film reviews, the concert ads, past ads for erotic services and "MWM seeks discreet." *For Rent. South Side. Studio and 1 BRs. W/w, eq., util. incl. A/C. Clean.*

There's still time, of course. Of course there is. How could there not be time?

A Piece in the Game

Alan Martinez

Play to win, play to play, getting played
we were so desperate to be happy
to make the right moves to be loved
our piece our stake in this dancing game

We watched too self-conscious, half-stupefied
by loneliness to rightly love your tight body, your ease
in that cage, except with sinking envy, and
there was, amidst all our yearning—*a secret scorn—*
too secret, perhaps, to be aware of

With a wavering movement, and emitting a tremulous
radiance, you danced shedding need, free of any love
save for this: a Schiaparelli silk scarf
unfurling fire red wings in your own azure sea—
rippling flesh is to spirit as heat is to flame—

With the air of forgotten divas, used to being looked at,
only now at this latest moment do you realize
looking out gazing in:
Whatever dream of love you've staked your piece on
must be found within our own sweet skin, or sought in vain

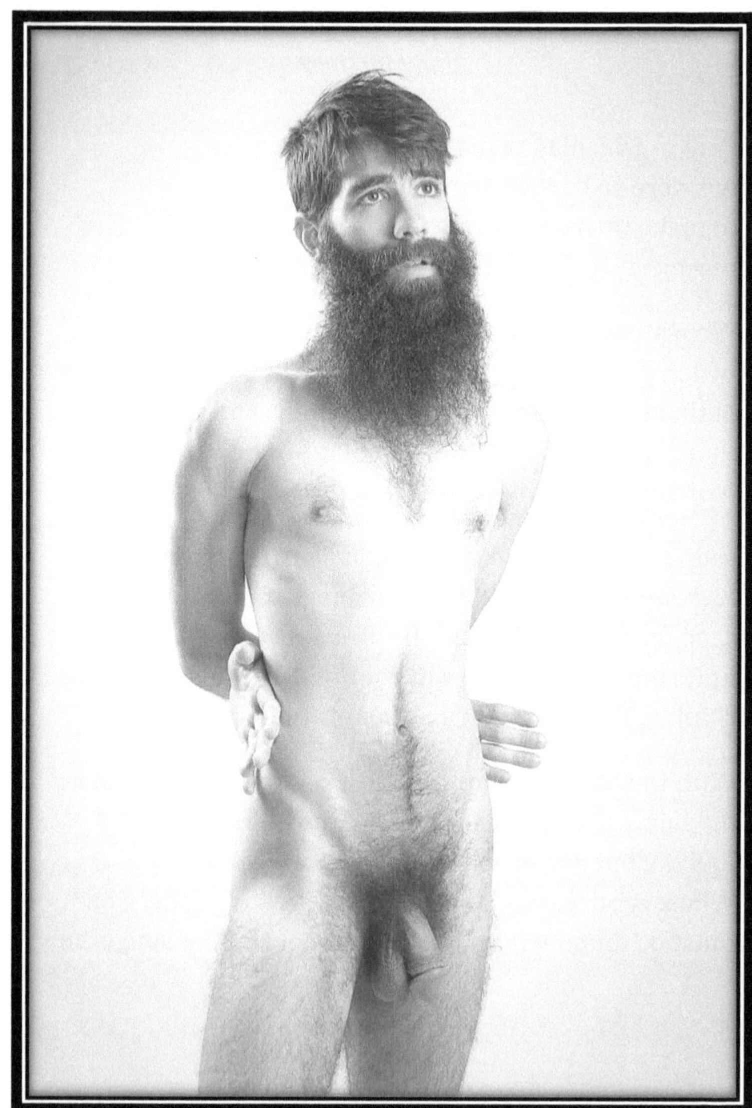

THREE HAIKU

Miodrag Kojadinović

1.

Lithe, hirsute, aloof
I stand in a stone-like twist,
your yogi, rav, priest.

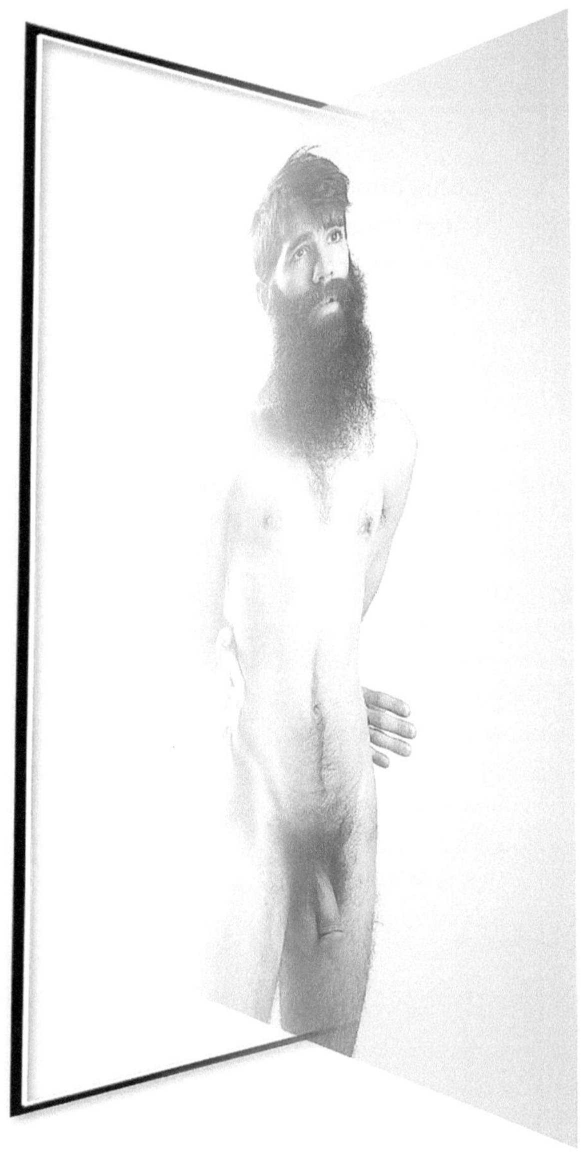

2.

No longer needed
seduction of cruel lens;
camera angle shifts.

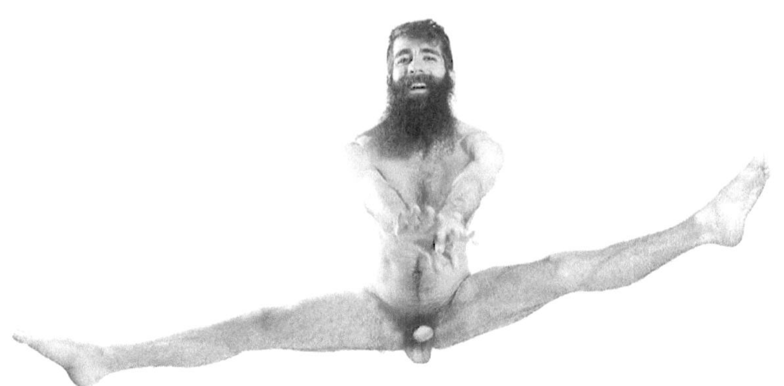

3.

Skyward I leap, nude,
my beard sways, my phallus throbs;
cosmos's fertilised.

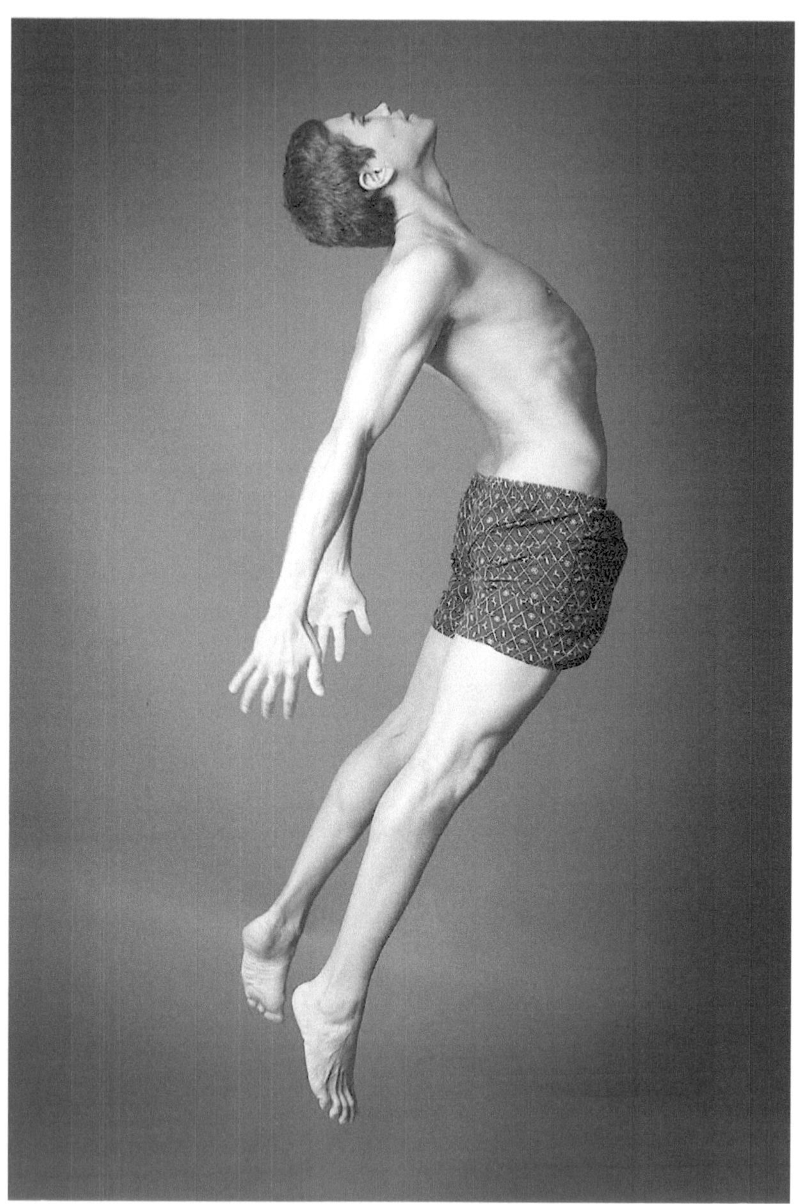

Kicks

Raymond Luczak

Some mornings when the mailroom's not so busy, I teach my boss Renee some more signs. Her signing's not too bad for a hearing person; if anything she's not afraid to use her face, especially when we talk about the guys in our lives, those we know and those we wish to have known. She's the only one who knows how much I want to be a famous model, something better than those *Playguy* pictures Davy had posed in the nude for; but I've never told her about him, even if he once was the only deaf model here in New York. I haven't seen him in quite some time since he was carried off to St. Vincent's. It's hard to believe it's already 1983, and I'm only twenty-four years old.

So we watch each other's diets, just making sure that she doesn't gain any more than what she has on now, and that I don't get flab on my stomach. I pick up rich guys a lot; it doesn't hurt that a whole lot of them think deaf guys are great in bed. Some of them worship the floor I walk on, and they shower gifts on me. What they don't know—or if they do, they don't acknowledge it—is that I'm theirs only for a time, but not for life. There's always someone else better, and with more money, waiting.

On my first day of working here, she had just tossed her banana peel over the mountainous stacks on her desk into her wastebasket when I came in, unsure of who Renee was. She pointed to the chair beside her desk and leaned forward a little; I was surprised at how easy it was to lip-read her. "Let Mother tell you something. I'm going to keep you here as long as I can because I want you to check out these boys for me." She leaned closer to me, and as she pointed to the traffic below her window, I smelled the fetid banana in her whisper. "I want to know how big they get."

Her conspiratorial looks often remind me of Davy when I first moved to New York a few years ago after quitting tech school upstate in Rochester. We'd met earlier that evening at a party, and then later that night he invited me to the Palladium.

I was very turned on by his fluttering around me; it was as if he was a moth attracted to the flame of my body. To this day I don't understand why he went off with some other guy, quite out of the blue: I suppose he had a bigger basket than I did.

From the window Renee and I make comments on the guys walking in and out of the lobby below, and when everything else drops to a standstill in the mailroom, we trade myths and true-story anecdotes about the guys we've slept with. She's had only four guys in her entire life, so I end up telling her a lot more than I should.

We look out the window again, and a man with a trimmed full beard from the eighth floor walks briskly into our building. "Such a pity."

"Married, right?"

"Yes. And for the third time." She holds up her *W* hand; she is the kind of signer that will always confuse the letter *W* with the number three.

"How do you know?"

"When you've been in here as long as I have, you pick up on those things. It's fun, kind of a game, just to figure out things. I do that when I'm bored." I laugh at her drollness, and we laugh even harder when she points out that she calls her best friend in California every day. Using her work phone to make long-distance calls is her biggest vice.

It's 11:52. She knows I like my lunch hours to be long because—well, why not? I leave with her telling me to be careful with the boys out there.

Here in Midtown a lot of cute guys go from office to deli, and from deli to drugstore, and from drugstore to office: Somehow this is more exciting than bars. There are no counters to lean against, and everyone is in constant motion. And so many of them are my type: close-cropped haircuts, clean-shaven chins, matching jacket and trousers, silk ties, Italian designer shoes, and smart watches. I have yet to meet a deaf guy who knows how to dress as well as I do.

So of course the ones with money are the thing: They never seem to know how to say no to pretty boys like me. I tell them

I don't have credit cards or a condo to my name, so they help pay my rent, take me out to all the new restaurants, and buy me the latest clothes. I never tell my deaf friends about this; they'd think I'm cheap. Besides they always complain about the number of older hearing guys willing to learn sign language compared to younger guys. Some of them are a little old, but at least they know how to spend money.

So for today I go south to the deli near Grand Central Station. I'm never that particular about delis, so I look for a short waiting line. I join it for Renee's order before I decide where to walk next. My eyes wander from street to line, storefront to corner, and businessman to . . .

The Guy.

He stands three places in front of me, and all my thoughts converge suddenly on his face. His brown eyes are bright as amber, his mustache outlines his thin upper lip but shows off his lower lip's slight pout, and his jaw is so smoothly shaven I want to brush the one freckle off below his short sideburn. The creamy darkness on his face shows how thick his beard can be. His aviator's leather jacket shelters his white shirt and navy blue tie from the February cold, and his blue chinos show snugness around his hips. I wonder how many pounds he can bench-press.

While the paunchy man curls his lips at the woman in front of The Guy, who can't decide on which cheeses she wants, I see The Guy fidget. His feet shift weight from one to the other, and his lips purse impatiently.

I cannot look at anything or anyone else; I may never see him again. I accumulate all his tiny, unconscious gestures like lint on a wet finger; with each one I fall for, they are never enough to satisfy me. I think about the color of his nipples. When he speaks, I try to lip-read him from the side.

"Ham . . . rye . . ."

What is he saying? I watch him drum his fingers on the counter as the surly man in his dirty apron slaps a cheddar slice atop the ham, its fat stripped clean.

Moving to the register, The Guy takes out his leather wallet, its edges whitened with age. As he removes a twenty, I see in the fold of his wallet no credit cards, only a New Jersey driver's license and a plastic stack of pictures. The woman at the counter gives him bills and change.

A minute later I order, "Ham on rye." I do not explain when Renee complains. The Guy must remain my secret; she knows too much about me already.

*

At the subway station I join the usual jam of people waiting to take the train downtown, weaving around women with smudged white Reeboks, striped terry socks over nylon stockings, duck head umbrellas and Danielle Steel library books, toward the front end of my train. I stand among men in their beige overcoats, serious hats and heavy maroon leather briefcases; not one of them returns my glances. They never care to go anywhere but home.

I look around at the ever-growing clusters of people, and I glance at a tall man. He's wearing a new motorcycle jacket, its waist belt left unbuckled, his pectorals tense and tight within his Gucci T-shirt. He must be one of those Brooklyn stallions who lives for the body, a real Marlon Brando type.

I move closer.

He looks up at me. Disgust dribbles all over his face: Is it my pearl earring or are my eyes so obvious?

I shrug and continue reading my *Village Voice*. I think about The Guy again and wonder what he must be thinking—now—on his way home: Does he have a Guy too on his mind? Probably not. It's possible that he has just married, and is absorbed in his own thoughts as most people on their way home seem to be. I wonder often what they think of—kids? mortgage payments? dinner plans? None of these possibilities belongs to me.

At last the train arrives but it is too full even to squeeze in, so I stand back to wait for the next one.

I look to my left; he has stood back too. I stare—for the hell of it—at him; after all, he can't avoid me as his eyes search for the next train.

I give a slight smile when I lift my chin slightly sideways. He aims his eyes past mine. I turn to see if the next train is mine. The wind whooshes from the other end; it's the uptown local. He seems to grunt.

I move even closer, blending into a cluster when he is not looking. I keep close to the back of the cluster, hoping that he will turn around and wonder where I've gone.

Now I am only a few feet away from him.

Our train comes slowly, packed like a can of sardines. I step into the half-foot-square space left behind him on the train; the subway doors close. He turns around to see who is behind him: His eyes spit disgust into mine. I try not to look too closely at the few lines on his supple neck. A lot of bull-faced guys have the softest necks.

As the train lurches forward, I smell the fading waves of impotent perfumes, *The New York Post*, and buttered popcorn. I glance down at the stallion's ass, and with a nonchalant expression, I let the back of my hand brush against it. He feels very solid. He shifts a little. I contemplate refolding my *Voice*; then he looks up at me with vicious eyes.

A black woman on one side of me moves, her elbow jarring into my back now and then. She tries to keep her bag on her shoulder but the straps seem very slippery; they are a cheap imitation red leather.

The train rocks before slowing down, and I bump into him. He braces his hand against the ceiling as I bend down to pick up my *Voice*, but he kicks it further away. I look up, about to ask just what the fuck why, only to find his eyes daring me to.

I decide not to bother with the *Voice*, and a smirk creeps onto The Bastard's face.

Well, he hasn't gotten my message . . .

The train lets out some people, and then heaves once more, downtown toward Astor Place and Bowling Green. My mind is so filled with a blank anger that the next time the doors open, I push him onto the platform just when the doors are about to close. I smile at him. I even lean down a little into the windows to wave back as he curses.

Others look at me, but they do not say anything.

*

Later that night I get a call from Alan, a mutual friend, about Davy's condition. He wants to know whether I will visit Davy or not. I don't know: They are not a family I'd choose.

So I tell him on my TTY machine: I DONT KNOW IM BUSY RIGHT NOW.

The only thing I leave out in my story to Renee is what a hunk The Bastard really was. She thinks I'm such a terrific storyteller with my face and gestures, and it always seems she can never stop laughing about the silliest details. If she passes me on the way to the restroom, she breaks into giggles that make her breasts look like Jell-O.

Sometimes the other mailroom boys ask with their eyes and faces, *Why is she laughing so loudly in there?* I shrug.

I am surprised to see The Bastard again at the subway station three days later. He has on the same jacket, and I happen to be wearing the same coat.

Today work was easy; there wasn't as much mail to cart around, and Renee stayed mostly out. And whenever she was in, she'd mimic her boss The Executive Slut as if she is Carol Channing: "Yes, I understand that you'd like your severance pay immediately, but you will have to wait out front until the check is ready. What was your last name again, please?" I know every word she says because she writes that kind of thing down on paper. She does it because she doesn't like it if I'm the only one there who's not laughing with the other guys. Renee says The Executive Slut had to sleep with the vice president—she calls him The One With No Dick At All—in order to be promoted way above three people who'd been here much longer than she had. So The Executive Slut she is.

As The Bastard swerves toward me, I wander aimlessly, as if I do not recognize him. Only in New York could I behave any way I want and not have to feel guilty.

He suddenly jabs me in my chest and says, "You don't touch guys like that!"

I sign, "Sorry-sorry, me not understand talk-talk."

"The hell you don't!" He kicks one side of my shin with his Zodiac cowboy boot, and saunters off coolly.

I limp after him and hide behind a beam; it seems those beams have those fresh NEW PAINT signs every other day.

I wait for our train to come. He lags behind a taller and older businessman getting on, but I do not slip aboard. While The Bastard struggles to squeeze in, I kick him in the ass. I am surprised at how soft it feels.

His face bangs against the businessman's back, and the older man's elbow jabs The Bastard's face in reflex. As the train doors close, he steams, alternating between curses at me and apologies to the disgruntled businessman. I notice the blackness of his middle fingernail as I flutter my eyelashes and blow him a kiss.

When his train finally leaves, I realize the throbbing pain in my shin.

I rest my leg on the sofa and watch a rerun of *Cosby*. I think of how nice it would be to be a part of a rich, deaf family, and to have a rich, deaf lover, perhaps someone like The Guy. I fall asleep to the throbbing ache of such dreams.

Everyone comes in late this morning; it must be one of those Mondays. I tell Renee about last Friday, which of course sends her off into a heaven of hysterics. Even The Executive Slut's glare cannot quiet her.

I wonder again whether I should tell her about The Guy, or about Davy dying, or about wanting to be a part of some family.

My excuse to The Executive Slut—that I bumped into my bed this morning—sends Renee off to the restroom.

The next day I wander painfully—my leg still hurting somewhat—up and down Lexington Avenue to see if The Guy would ever return. I monitor the deli from a variety of viewpoints, different corners and nearby gourmet stands, as if I am waiting for someone to meet me.

Finally he arrives with a dark scowl plastered on his face. As he walks past, he looks up as if something in the window behind me has distracted him.

I look down and berate myself instantly for turning away. As he joins the line outside the deli, he gives me a look of puzzlement.

The lunch hour traffic eats away at my patience. I look at my watch every twenty seconds, then back at the deli window where I can see him.

The Guy steps out finally with a white bag of what I imagine to be something like a ham and cheddar sandwich on rye, no seeds. As he walks back, I think of how much I need to piss; but he stops in front of me and says, "Is something the matter?"

I mouth my words slowly and carefully. "No. I'm fine."

He gives me the same look as before—I am used to this kind of reaction from those who expect me to speak—and continues north on Lexington. I blend into the crowds, following him to the corner of 47th and Lexington where I loiter. He walks east past Third Avenue; I'll cover that next time.

I return to work early. Renee says, "Scott, are you all right?"

I shake my head. "No. I'm tired of working here."

Renee's hands fly to her hips. "How do you think I feel after working here for twenty-six years?" She leaves when the U.P.S. man shows up with his clipboard.

The next morning The Bastard is poised outside the token booth at the subway station. I recognize him from the escalator, and I steel myself against the pain of my limp. A cop with a panda's stomach stands watch near the exit doors; I am relieved to see him there, even if he is ugly with a stalk-like pimple on one side of his reddish neck.

People mill about me as I walk toward the street entrance. I do not give The Bastard any glint of recognition as I follow closely behind a woman in an ermine coat.

As I walk past the cop, The Bastard yells, "That's the queer I was tellin' you . . ." At least that is what I think I've heard, but my ears are hardly 100% accurate.

I continue walking on ahead. There is a sudden tremor of feet running after me. I turn to find the cop looking at me, and then at The Bastard. I sign, "Sorry-sorry, me deaf. Wrong-wrong?"

"He kicked me on the train."

I indicate lip-reading is a difficult art, which is true for most people anyhow.

"What?"

I make my voice crack like a scratchy record and sign at the same time.

"I kicked *you* on the train? Yes I did, you touched my ass. You fags make me sick!"

I storm off, forgetting the sharp pain in my leg.

Renee thinks this even funnier, and The Executive Slut gives me a look suggesting I should be quarantined with Renee. My boss has taken to calling me Smart-Ass Scott.

Alan calls me to invite me to a small get-together brunch with his friends after visiting Davy together. I think how nice it would be, but I know these people. They never talk about anything else but who has died, who might get it next, and how they'd handle it if they got it. I say on my TTY machine: IM SORRY BUT IM REALLY BUSY.

I stay away from the deli for two days, but by Friday I have to see The Guy again. The pain in my leg is almost gone, and I wander about on 47th Street. Half a block ahead is The Guy, turning south on Lexington.

I join the line in the deli without thinking whether I should or not. The Guy is six places ahead of me, but as he turns around he recognizes me. He smiles a little, but turns to stare at the menu above the counter. He leaves the deli without looking back.

A week later I see The Bastard again, this time across the street from the deli. It is slightly warmer now. With spring barely blossoming above the sidewalks and with The Guy on my mind so much, I have forgotten about The Bastard's build. People brushing by carry lunches in tiny Saks' Fifth Avenue bags, strained Duane Reade plastic bags, and battered leather attachés.

As he runs up to me, his eyes burn like the sun's smoking ray in a magnifying glass and I am a matchbook underneath. "You're not going anywhere, are ya?" I can hear enough to know this is a statement.

"You are very wrong." I try to swerve around him, but he grabs my bag and takes Renee's lunch out. It is a plastic tray filled with radishes, green peppers, and other salad greens with three tiny containers of Ranch dressing; she could never get enough of that stuff.

He unsnaps it open. "No you don't. Eat!"

I pretend to be about to pour on the dressing, but I jerk it instead into his eyes. It drips like paint on his leather jacket as I leap into a run.

At Lexington and 48th, I turn left and sneak into a spacious lobby. As I pace my breathing on the escalator, I look back. Nothing.

I return to the mailroom twenty-five minutes late; I leave Renee's new salad on her counter.

Later Renee stands in front of me. "Why didn't you tell Mother you got back home?"

Sometimes I hate her way of talking. If I were hearing, I'd probably hate her even more and work elsewhere for better money.

"You found someone and you two went at it like squirrels and you just got back from his place or what?"

I give her a look of exasperation.

"I thought we got along good, you know, like good friends."

I wonder why I even bother to tell her anything.

"Scott, you're not very smart." She looks around, and in a lower voice, she says, "The Executive Slut was looking for you. Let Mother tell you something. You can't always be late. Because. If. You. Do. You. Will. Get. Fired. So take those packages up to the eleventh floor."

As I enter the down escalator at the station, I suddenly sense someone familiar behind me. The Bastard smiles with the sleeve of my jacket already in his vise. "Goin' home just now, huh?" He shoves me a little as we step off the escalator and pins me against a beam on the platform. Bystanders watch us with bored eyes as he pulls my collar against the beam.

"Fag." He turns around and notices the bystanders. "Look at this fag here—"

I suddenly ram my knee up against his basket. Yowling out in pain, he makes a move to grab me again, but I am already off. I look back, and he is bending over, the veins vivid against his neck and a hand over his crotch.

Renee will never know about this.

The next few nights I get nightmares. The Bastard has been stalking the bars with a gleaming switchblade in his hand; he finds me dancing with The Guy, who happens to be a deaf millionaire's son so he knows signs; we've already planned a vacation in the Bahamas. The only thing left for us to do will come after the dancing: the answer that leads from the question to the bed. But The Bastard steps between us, and he rips my shirt apart with its few buttons popping. Plunging his knife into me, he whispers clearly enough: "Now, that's a lesson for you."

And then this: The Bastard hires a private investigator who finds out where I live. With that address in hand, The Bastard goes and waits next to my mailbox in my building. There are variations of our struggle in the lobby, but the end remains the same: I die with no one else hearing my last gasps for help. I wake up early and think of any other last things I need to do short of following one of those *How to Write Your Own Will* guides.

I check the back of the new *Voice* to see if The Bastard has left any warnings there for me. There are none: It is as if I do not exist.

I sit with the *Post* spread out in front of me. I am early, and Renee doesn't even arrive until 8:30. Time passes as I force myself to read its lurid scandals all the way through.

Renee taps on my head lightly. "Was the party last night so good that you came straight to work?"

I jolt. "No . . ."

"Mmm. You'll have to tell Mother what's wrong."

"No, no."

She walks around my desk and pulls me off my chair and squeezes me. I feel smothered by her soft flesh. "Now, honey, you've got Mother right here, so tell me what's wrong, mmm?"

"Please, please. Not here. Not at work."

"We can eat out for lunch."

I shake my head vehemently.

She gives me a look that means, *We're in for a long day.*

Yet I keep thinking of The Guy, and how he will save me from The Bastard, and how I really will have to tell someone other than Renee who thinks everything I say is funny, or has to be funny. But how can I trust another deaf person if they gossip so much in detail about Davy's sex life? And about who he might've gotten it from?

I hurry so fast that I don't realize I'm right behind The Guy. It's been suddenly chilly today so it is easy to imagine his warmth. He turns around and says, "Something the matter or what?"

I shake my head in reflex, and remembering my resolution to be more upfront, I nod.

"Hey, you! The usual?" It is the churlish man again.

"Yeah." He turns back to me. "You wanna talk about it?"

"Hey, you!" The man barks at me. "What d'ya want?"

I mouth slowly and point out what I want: "Ham and cheddar on rye, no seeds." The man nods and pulls my order together deftly.

The Guy looks at me. "You just ordered the same thing as me."

"I'm sorry."

After we leave the deli, The Guy gestures his bag toward Burger King. "We can go inside there."

We clear our table of its scattered salt and torn ends of straw wrappers. He opens his bag and begins chomping away on his sandwich.

Between bites he says, "Well, eat."

"I can't."

"Why not?"

"Why do you want to listen to me?"

"Well . . . it so happens that you look like you need a girl."

I shake my head and take a deep breath. "I think I'm in love with you." I feel again the rare clarity of my own speech: I feel for once as if I am hearing.

He turns red, almost coughing on his bite and yet chewing. "I can't understand that kind of thing, y'know what I mean?"

I nod, my lips turning tense and tight and taut.

He wraps up his sandwich and drops it back into his bag. "Sorry, pal."

I take a bite from my sandwich. Ham and cheddar tastes putrid in my mouth, and I stuff it into a trash bin.

While I finish sorting the mail for tomorrow's first delivery, I find Renee hasn't budged from her counter, still chattering away on the phone with her mother. She told me once that she'd sometimes leave long-distance cryptic messages on her friends' answering machines, and they'd either have to wait for her next call or call her themselves. "It's a game, kinda fun," she said; somehow she hasn't lost a friend yet.

When she sees me in my jacket, she waves me over and covers the receiver with her hand. "Going home now? Mother needs you here." She points to the seat beside her desk. I resign myself to watching from her window as workers run toward the subway. Some go by very fast, even in their high heels.

A new thought chills me: What if The Bastard catches me in this window? I sit back, but I find I cannot just lean back and relax as I'd always done when we're alone. Even The Executive Slut is going home early for once. I pull my sock up; it is then Renee says, "Bye, kissy-kissy poo-poo."

She looks over. "That's a nice sock you have. What brand is it?" She writes the word BRAND down.

"That's not a brand. You ask which designer." I write the word down.

"I'm sorry, okay?" She lifts her hands in exasperation. "I don't know what else I can do. I thought if you needed help, you'd ask me . . . I know it's got to be some man on your mind, and it's not fun anymore, right? You in love? Well?"

"I can't explain."

"Are you in a hurry?"

I nod.

"We can eat out if you want."

"God forbid."

"Now that sounds more like Smart Scott."

I do not even smile.

"You know I miss him. What happened?" She says this very quietly.

I head for the elevators.

Dropping a token into the turnstile, I leap down the grimy steps toward my train's platform. When I slow down, I'm amazed I should feel so free now in this place.

I look around, but The Bastard is nowhere to be seen. As I walk to the place where the front car of my train will stop, he steps out from behind a beam and pulls my collar to his chest and drags me near the wall under the grimy staircase. He slams me against it, and its hardness stings my shoulder blades and tailbone. I feel like a floppy doll in his hands as he throttles me again. "Huh? Huh!"

I look past him to see if The Guy will ever show up. The taste of ham and cheddar on rye, no seeds, rises in my mouth.

I scream to the best of my ability, "Go ahead, fuck me all you want, I got nothing to live for!" My stomach feels queasy, ready to heave.

A look of surprise crosses his face. He walks away, past onlookers with their books and papers. I avert my eyes from their faces, watching instead a sewer rat nosing a candy wrapper. It skitters away when the train comes.

Two hours later I sit with Oscar, from among the better ones in my stable of rich men, in a pasta restaurant on West 58th Street; he is sixty years old. Although it takes him forever to get it up, he is fond of French-kissing me. When he turns amorous behind his bedroom door off Central Park West, I close my eyes and fantasize about someone else. It is the only way I can come, and they never ask. Besides, my deafness makes it hard for them to ask me those questions they want to ask the most; their inquisitive glances roll off my shoulders like piffled raindrops.

But Oscar is very nice; he knows how to put clothes together, and shops only at Saks' and Bergdorf Goodman's; he even has his own tailor. He is not very good with sign language, but he does try to communicate with gestures and an occasional scribble on a notepad. Tonight I have ordered spinach linguini enveloped in a creamy wine sauce and a cluster of sautéed mushrooms; at twenty dollars, it had better be exquisite.

As I light another cigarette I notice a quartet of deaf men entering and taking a larger round table near the rear; I am relieved I do not know them. They are wearing jeans, Izods, and deck shoes; their hands do not know how to talk in a well-mannered and tempered way. As I watch their conversation, I feel ashamed that they should talk boldly about sex and how one could die from it, and I know it will not be long before Davy's name will crop up. It does, and then I turn my attention to the plate before me.

Oscar speaks slowly, "Do you know them?"

I shake my head no.

That night I dream I have become an old man, wearing a toupee and plastered sideburns, in a pink Cadillac cruising the condemned warehouses of Alphabet City. Off one corner, I catch through the open door of a pool hall a group of older deaf guys talking and laughing and playing cards while two beer-gutted guys outside the doorway nudge each other, pointing to my car with their aluminum cans. The shorter one mumbles something, and they break into raucous laughter.

As I drive away, I suddenly remember I have met these two a long time ago.

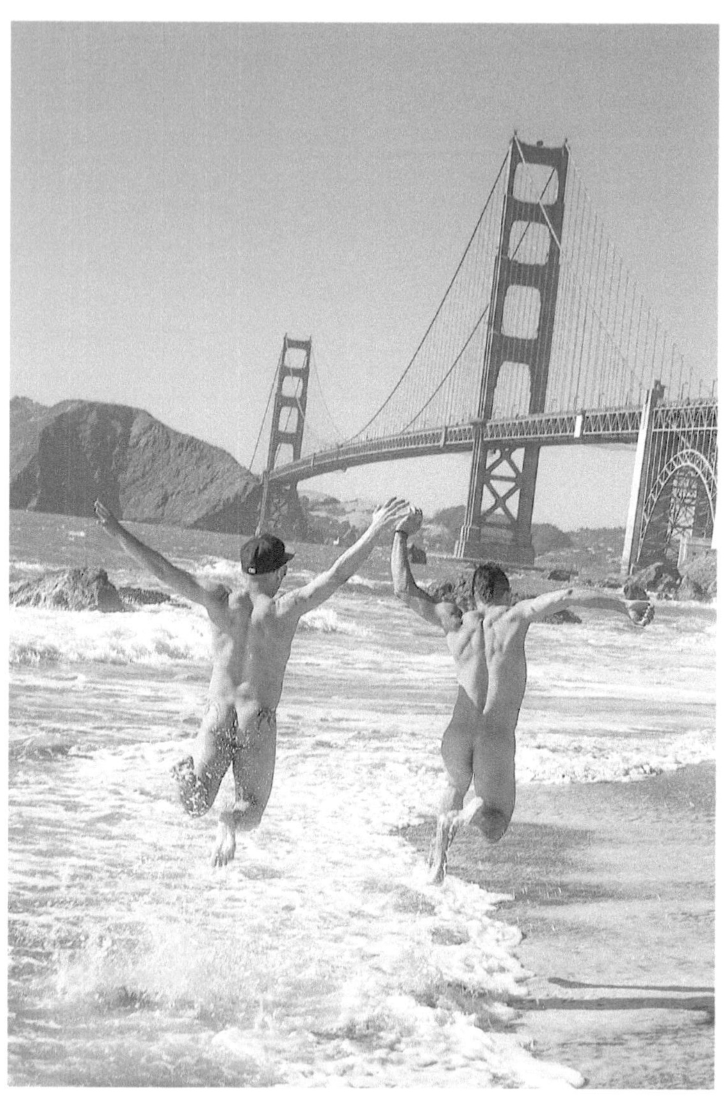

Limerick

Mike McClelland

Limerick. The name itself was a joke, a riddle, and that was how it treated itself. If you were to strip the magic and mystery, the sex and intoxication away from Limerick, it was nothing more than two interconnected garages in Russian Hill, far from the Castro and the rest of San Francisco's nightlife. One garage had a large stage, the other a bar. The floors were cement but covered with heaps of dusty overlapping Persian rugs that hadn't been clean even when they'd first been placed. The walls were wooden, painted deep red, and accented with an assortment of mismatched candelabras, refilled each night with fresh off-white tapers, lit in what seemed to be a blatant fuck-you to fire code. The lighting was low and the air smoky, and it seemed to belong in the 1920s rather than the early 2000s. Low couches lined the walls and corners in order to encourage confessions and seductions while a mishmash of bar tables filled the remainder of the open space. The music played low and quiet on a scratchy antique phonograph.

The bar was lorded over by Butler Fay, which was not his real name. Butler owned Limerick and dressed in an assortment of sparkling caftans despite his obviously muscular physique. He had kohl-lined eyes and a slick, slender mustache that he curled at the edges. Outwardly, he was meaner than a snake, but engendered nothing but loyalty and devotion. The stage belonged to Butler's "Devils," a team of seven featured male dancers. Four go-go boys provided back up and occasionally poured shots into the mouths of those closest to the stage, their uniformly large pectoral muscles squeezing as they dripped libations into eager, open mouths.

One particular Friday night, Limerick was packed with men of all shapes and sizes—and a few women—all lured in by word-of-mouth. On stage under Limerick's one electric light, a heavy brass spotlight, were Sion and Croix, two of Butler's Devils. They frequently shared the stage, and more frequently, a bed. Their performance on this night was a tango with Sion in black tights, a rose in his mouth, and Croix in miniscule red shorts and red heels, expertly twisting, clapping, and writhing to the sharp sounds of "El Dia Que Me Quieras" scratching out of the phonograph.

*

It was August of 2003 and Jamie had been dancing at Limerick for six months. He loved every bit of it: the other go-go boys, the Devils, and even Butler, who was an asshole but a sweet asshole. Most of all he loved the atmosphere: the candlelight, the record music, and the focus on performance.

Jamie's entire life had been about performance. He'd come to San Francisco to be a Corps Dancer for the San Francisco Ballet and had excelled beyond even his own high expectations. He could see a clear line to being Principle. Brian Mans, who had been Principle for years, was approaching retirement, and Jamie had doubled down, desperate to be the best dancer at the ballet by the time that happened. He'd begun to feel pain in the shin of his right leg but was able to dance through it without any signs of weakness, so he told himself it couldn't be much of a problem. It had been a problem. What had been a stress fracture became compound in practice, the bone piercing through his skin in the middle of rehearsal.

Jamie taught classes for a while after that, his leg put back together with metal pins and rods, but he couldn't stand to be near ballet. He felt like his destiny had been taken from him. He felt like he'd been punished for working hard.

He had stumbled into Limerick one day on his way to his apartment in Nob Hill, an apartment that was quickly becoming far out of his price range. He saw a group of well-dressed men walking up the steps to a Russian Hill apartment and had assumed they were going to a party at a friend's house. He hated himself for being envious, but all of his friends had been with the ballet and his relationships with them had all broken along with his leg. He was about to turn and continue up the road when an energetic, curly-haired redhead walked by and caught him looking at the apartment.

"Have you been in?" the redhead asked, his green eyes wide.

"No, I don't know who lives there," Jamie said. He felt the need to explain himself, to declare he hadn't been spying. "I was just daydreaming."

The ginger smiled. "If you really want to dream, go up to the door, knock, and tell the guy at the door 'Madeleine Elster' when he asks you for the password. I'm meeting some friends there later so maybe I'll see you there."

With that, the ginger winked and continued up the hill.

That's how Jamie and Limerick had found each other, and they'd been together nearly every night since. Jamie had quickly befriended Butler, who reminded him of a ballet dancer: theatrical and vicious but fiercely loyal and loving. Within a few days he had convinced Butler to let him audition to be a go-go boy, but the Devils were a different story. Butler didn't hire new Devils and none of the current ones said how they'd gotten the job. Butler did, however, love Jamie's dancing, particularly his limp. Butler wanted every element of Limerick to be unique and noticeable, and a limping go-go boy apparently counted.

On that Friday night, Jamie was struggling to concentrate on his own dancing, as Sion and Croix's performance center stage was incredibly stimulating. Whenever the Devils did duos or trios the results were explosive. He scanned the audience in an effort to find something else to focus on. The room was packed, couches and bar tables full and standing room nonexistent.

As Jamie danced and surveyed the room, he noticed a dark-featured guy out of the corner of his eye, watching him. He was sitting in profile, his left side facing Jamie but his head, which was covered by a black and red baseball cap, was turned towards the stage. His tight black T-shirt and even tighter jeans left little to the imagination. He had a muscular body and a butt to die for, its heft propped up by the barstool. Jamie watched as the guy looked down at his drink, swirled it around, then brought his eyes back up to the stage, his eyes meeting Jamie's. Jamie felt a flush of heat and turned back to Sion and Croix. They were just finishing up and Jamie focused on supporting them, dancing in time with their moves, providing a bass to their intoxicating treble.

When the song finished, Jamie and the other go-go boys held out hats to collect tips for the main act. The noise level rose in the small space as the polite crowd turned their attention from the performance to each other. Every minute or so, Jamie stole a glance at the guy in the ball cap, who was staring at him more shamelessly now. He'd turned the cap around, making his face more visible. His face was tough; he had a big square jaw and dark, intense eyes. Jamie winked at him and the guy smiled broadly.

Jamie considered going to talk to him between acts. Butler didn't like the dancers talking to the patrons, and he practically forbade anything beyond talking, but Butler was busy at the bar. Jamie could slip over, get the guy's number, and be back to the stage before anyone noticed. He shot a look at the guy's butt again and decided to risk it.

Just as Jamie was setting off to meet this mysterious man, a hand grabbed his shoulder. Jamie looked down at the hand and saw a set of long, fake fingernails painted in leopard spots.

"Butler," he smiled, turning to face his boss.

"Jamie, darling, you're up next."

Jamie searched Butler's expertly mascaraed eyes for a hint of sarcasm, but found them honest, an unusual look on Butler.

"What do you mean, 'you're up?'" he asked. "Is someone hurt?"

"No, I just want you to dance," Butler said, not bothering to hide that he was already bored with the conversation.

Jamie wasn't willing to buy it so easily. He was too used to disappointment to believe that Butler was giving him a chance to be a Devil.

"What about Mink?" he asked.

Mink's performance had been scheduled to follow Sion and Croix's tonight and Jamie had been looking forward to it, as it called for them all to dress as wild animals, which was a look that always garnered plenty of tips.

Butler sighed heavily and pulled on each end of his mustache, a sure sign he was frustrated. "He'll go *after* you! This isn't the Royal Shakespeare Company; I can mix up my fucking program! Just get ready. I assume you have something ready?"

Of course Jamie had *something ready*. He'd had something ready since that first day he'd stumbled into Limerick and decided that he had to work there.

"You bet, boss. When I am on?"

Butler tilted his head and delivered his bitchiest smile.

"Five minutes," he said. He turned and strutted back to the bar, his silver caftan swaying behind him, candlelight shooting off it like a mirrored ball.

*

Kenny watched the dancers on Limerick's stage and couldn't help feeling envy. He'd always wanted to dance. He'd learned ballet and jazz from his sisters as a youngster even though his father wouldn't let him take classes. Later, as a teenager, he'd hit the clubs and discovered that he was pretty good at hip-hop. But then duty had called. Now he was back from Afghanistan, where he'd been on tour for eighteen months. He told his family he was home on leave, but the truth was he'd been discharged. Honorably, so no one would ask. Don't Ask, Don't Tell, but he could still barely admit that to himself.

Kenny had a red and black Chicago Bulls cap pulled low on his forehead in order to conceal his face. He was so used to hiding that he didn't yet feel comfortable being out in the open, even though the worst that could happen had already happened.

His attempt to keep his face concealed, however, was being sabotaged by his eyes' absolute need to stare at the go-go dancer on the far left side of the stage. Kenny appreciated the tango happening center stage, but something about the go-go dancer made his mouth dry, his stomach tight. The dancer was wearing tight, short jean shorts and black sneakers. His bare chest was smooth, and oiled, as were his legs and arms. He was muscular but lithe, like a ballet dancer. He was doing the same movements as the other go-go boys, vamping and hopping in support of the tangoing duo, but his movements were far more graceful and silent. The dancer had very strong features, a sharp nose and high cheekbones. His face was slim and intense, his lips full and curled, his eyes focused straight ahead. Kenny had been watching him so closely that he'd even noticed something slightly amiss with the dancer's right leg, a small hitch or limp with his movements. It made him sexier, more real.

Kenny was attracted to graceful men. Men with complicated faces and strong features. Men who were liquid with their movement, who could curl around him and make him forget anyone else had ever existed. Men who didn't let the world weigh them down, who kept their shoulders high, their postures strong. This dancer was like that and Kenny couldn't stop watching.

Kenny wasn't at all like that. He felt simultaneously strong and useless. At once naïve and know-it-all, worldly and sheltered. He was strong because he was supposed to be. Kenny watched the dancer move and thought about how every muscle on the dancer's body was meant for something, and he loved the utility of that, the natural beauty of it. The candlelight caught all the shadows of the dancer's body and made him look like bottled fire. Kenny looked down at his Jack Daniels and then back up and just caught the dancer's eye before he swung his head back to the duo at the center of the stage. The hairs stood up on Kenny's arms and his mouth went dry.

He couldn't look away. He turned his hat around and stared blatantly at the dancer, hoping he'd look his way again. When the dancer did, Kenny kept his eyes right on him, even though his cheeks burned and his palms got sweaty. He wanted the dancer to know he wanted him. The dancer was collecting tips, bending over and smiling at people swiftly and gracefully. Kenny considered taking some money up to the stage but he didn't want to lose his seat. He knew there were more acts up, and if the dancer was going to stay in the same place on stage Kenny wanted to keep the view he had.

When he'd finished collecting tips, the dancer looked up again. He caught Kenny's eye and winked, his sharp face softening instantly. Kenny wished he could think of something sexy to do, but his natural reaction happened to be a giant smile—and a hard on.

For a second, it looked as if the dancer would head his way. Then the bartender swooped up behind him and started talking. They had a short conversation, and afterwards the dancer was smiling distractedly, no longer looking at Kenny. The bartender was very attractive, in a gender-bendy kind of way, and Kenny wondered if he and the dancer were involved outside the workplace.

Damn it, he thought. He cursed himself for not going up to the stage while the dancer had been collecting tips. The dancer disappeared through a door behind the stage and Kenny worried, absurdly, that he was meeting the bartender out back for a romantic rendezvous. As if it was his business.

Kenny nursed his Jack Daniels, waiting for the next dance. Even if nothing else was going to come of it, he was happy to just watch a while longer. There was something about the dancing that turned his mind off and allowed him to relax, to forget about the present, and worse, the future.

After a few minutes, the bartender appeared on stage. Kenny scanned the back to see if the dancer had returned. He hadn't, but the three other go-go boys had, taking their places on stage. Each wore white tights and a set of feathery white angel wings. But where was *his* dancer?

The bartender spoke, as he had before the other dances this evening. "You're all in for quite the treat! We have a debut Devil this evening, though he *is* a familiar face and *comes* with *loads* of experience. Since this is, in a way, an audition, he doesn't have an official Devil name yet. But suggestions are welcome, provided he doesn't fall on his face." The bartender cast a glance over his shoulder and then turned back to the audience. "So, without further ado, here is our Jamie, with a new take on the dance between the witch Odile and Prince Siegfried from *Swan Lake*."

Kenny watched as the dancer from before, Jamie, came through the rear door and took to the stage. He was wearing long black tights and was shirtless aside from a large black wing that soared out from his left side, held on by a harness that wrapped around his chest. His face was masked black around his eyes with a beak jutting out above his mouth. He was easily identifiable by his lips, to Kenny at least, who had been staring at them for some time.

Jamie was wearing a black ballet shoe on his left foot while his other foot was bare. He held a crutch, painted white, in his arms. He looked straight ahead, his eyes black under the mask. Kenny could see how controlled his breath was, slow and deliberate, filling and leaving his impressive body in measured doses. The record player started to play a piece of string music, presumably from *Swan Lake*, and Jamie began to move around the stage, holding the crutch out toward the audience like a magician showing the audience a dove before making it disappear. The go-go dancers stood one on either side and one in the back, creating a triangle around him. They began slowly to perform ballet moves as if they were standing at a *barre*. They each performed a different set of moves and it created a striking visual, with Jamie in black at the center of their white triangle.

Once Jamie had dramatically shown the crutch to the audience and his dancers had begun their slow, formal dance, he began dancing himself, using the crutch as a partner. Placing it in the center of the stage, he held himself out from it, pushing himself up onto his one shoed foot until he was on the very tip, his arm stretched flat out to the top of the crutch.

From there, Jamie burst into a frenetic mix of ballet and tumbling, supported amply by the energetic go-go boys. Like the tango, it was formal, but also sexy and funny. While he'd been initially serious, as he continued to dance a huge smile spread across Jamie's face. Laughs rang out through the audience as he used his crutch to support himself while simultaneously doing a plié and chugging a cocktail handed to him by one of the go-go boys. He didn't seem to take himself too seriously, which was probably a necessity of being a limping-danseur-go-go boy.

Kenny couldn't take his eyes off of Jamie. Every slight shift of the dancer's taut, languid muscles made him feel breathless. As the music reached a crescendo, Jamie once again launched himself up onto the point of his left foot, spinning expertly. When he stopped, he was completely still, staring straight ahead, right at Kenny. Jamie blew a kiss right at him and Kenny just stared, mesmerized. Without realizing it, he'd broken into a big, dumb grin. He cursed himself, wishing he'd done something sexier. But it was too late; Jamie bowed to the cheering crowd and walked off the stage without looking back.

*

Jamie saw the guy in the baseball cap staring at him as he danced, and it was an incredible turn-on. He'd been nervous when he first took the stage, but when he saw the guy's dark eyes shamelessly plastered on him, taking in every inch of his body, Jamie relaxed. He felt like he was dancing just for him, whoever this guy was, and it allowed him to let loose.

Butler was always telling all of them—the Devils and the go-go boys—that they needed to be funny and sexy when they danced.

"If people wanted serious, they'd be at the damned ballet, not here," he'd said to Jamie right before he'd stepped onto the Limerick stage for the first time as a go-go boy. It had stung then. Wasn't Jamie *supposed* to be on the stage of the ballet?

As he took the stage for the first time tonight as a Devil, he felt nervous, rigid. Like he'd felt in the ballet, where he'd used his nerves to remain focused. But he knew he had to loosen up. And when he saw the guy in the cap, his eyes running up and down Jamie's body, it made him feel free. Free to mess up, to joke around, to be sexy. A danseur in the ballet was a beautiful thing, but he was often there in support of a ballerina, allowing her to shine. Now, Jamie was the star of the show, and he loved it.

When he finished his performance, he spontaneously decided to blow the guy in the cap a kiss. It felt childish, but he felt like he owed the guy something, and he wanted his attention. Jamie found him in the crowd and blew him a kiss, nice and slow, and he loved the way the brooding, serious-looking guy's eyes widened and his mouth curled into a big, toothy grin in response.

Jamie exited the stage and went out the back door, which led to a small dressing room. Mink was in there, strapping himself into a fur loincloth.

Mink gave Jamie a kiss on the cheek.

"Awesome job, baby. Welcome to the Devils."

"Thanks. Do you think it went all right?"

"Well, I only had the rear view, but the rear view was pretty spectacular." He slapped Jamie on the ass.

Mink continued, "Butler told me to ask you to wait here, he'll be back in a second to talk to you. I've got to get out there. We're running behind schedule because of our new *prima ballerina*."

He winked and headed out the door. Jamie heard Butler introduce Mink, and shortly afterwards the door swung open and the owner strutted in. He was talking excitedly before the door was even shut.

"Beautiful! Just beautiful, you flaming asshole. I knew you could dance, but who knew you were so good with a crutch! Wait. A beautiful dancer *and* good on crutches? I've got your name. You're going to be Kerrigan. Like Nancy Kerrigan! Get it?"

"No you will not!" Jamie laughed, giving him a fake punch in the shoulder. "Does that mean you'll let me do it again?"

"Consider your audition passed. And take the rest of the night off. Or morning—how the *hell* is it already three-thirty in the morning? This is what happens when I drink Red Bull. And when I open at midnight. Shit, now I've got to find myself a new go-go boy. Let me know if you can think of anyone who'd be a good *fit*."

As he said "fit" he slapped Jamie on the ass and sailed out of the room. That was as flirty as Butler got. Though Jamie was sure any of the dancers, himself included, would have been willing to get a little *closer* to Butler, their boss had a strict policy of not getting involved with his employees. Which Jamie respected.

Jamie changed out of his costume and into jeans and a tank top. He replaced his single pointe shoe with his black Nikes and slipped through the door, back into the performance room. No one spotted him; Mink was at the point of his performance where he "hunted" the go-go boys, which involved a lot of very suggestive wrestling moves, and everyone's eyes were glued to that.

Jamie worked his way around the stage and into the audience area. Immediately, he spotted the guy in the ball cap, who was watching the performance on stage. Jamie didn't think his eyes looked as interested in Mink as they had in him, but he worried that he was imagining that. Still, he was riding a post-performance high. He wove through the crowd to the guy's table and stood beside him.

It only took the guy a second to notice Jamie's presence. His eyes slid from the stage to Jamie, and as soon as he saw him he smiled wide.

"Hey," he said, his voice low and smoky. "Great job up there."

Jamie held out his hand. "Thanks. I'm Jamie."

The guy offered a firm and formal handshake. "I'm Kenny."

Jamie was getting a bit nervous. This guy, Kenny, was as smooth and confident in person as his eyes were from across the room. Jamie knew he had to act now or he'd lose his nerve. He also wanted to get out of there before Butler spotted him fraternizing with the clientele.

"Hey, Kenny, I've got the rest of the night off. Well, morning. Do you want to get out of here? Grab a cup of coffee?"

Kenny's smile grew wider and turned wolfish.

"That sounds perfect," he said, his eyes slowing rolling down Jamie's body.

*

Kenny followed Jamie out a side door of the bar and up a flight of cement stairs. He kept his eyes glued on Jamie's insanely sculpted butt as they ascended. He found himself hoping for another staircase.

They emerged right onto Van Ness, which didn't seem geographically possible.

"Isn't the front door on Bonita? How'd we get over here?" he asked.

"Don't question it. I'm convinced Butler has some kind of magic on the place. Did you notice how much bigger it seems on the inside than it looks from the outside?"

"I did wonder about that," Kenny said, distracted, disappointed to no longer be face-level with Jamie's ass.

"I think that place was a gin joint way back when. So it looks like a set of garages from outside but it stretches down and back quite a ways," Jamie said, leading the way up Van Ness toward Fort Mason.

Kenny followed along. "Why is it in Russian Hill, and not the Castro? It would bring in a fortune there."

"Butler, the bartender, also owns the place. He inherited a ton of money from somewhere and bought the buildings there. I don't think he needs the money, and he wanted it in Russian Hill because of *Tales of the City*, I think. Or maybe *Vertigo.* Or both. The story changes every time he tells it," Jamie said, laughing.

Kenny thought Jamie's laugh sounded nervous, which made him excited. He liked getting signs that he was flustering this gorgeous, graceful man. He stopped and grabbed Jamie's shoulder, turning him to face him. They were close to the same height. Jamie was slimmer and a bit taller, while Kenny was more solid.

"Do you want to get coffee, or should we get to know each other a little better than that?" he said, shameless.

Jamie's eyes widened in surprise and Kenny thought he noticed red sneak onto the dancer's cheeks under the streetlight. He looked lost for words for a second, so Kenny decided to make the first move. He stepped in and kissed Jamie, wrapping his arms around the dancer's strong shoulders. It was a slow kiss, and he inhaled as their lips touched, relishing Jamie's salty, athletic scent. Their lips met perfectly and the kiss was light and exploratory, almost curious. But also electric.

After a moment, Kenny pulled back, hoping he'd convinced Jamie.

"My place or yours?" he asked, optimistic.

Jamie smiled, kissed him again quickly, and said, "I can't sleep with you."

*

Jamie watched as Kenny's expression changed from interest to confusion. He felt awful. He wanted to sleep with Kenny. God, he wanted to *everything* with Kenny. He wanted to spend days getting lost in every inch of that hot, muscled body.

Their kiss had been amazing. He'd been surprised by Kenny's restraint. He'd assumed, from the way he'd been eye-fucking him all night, that Kenny would be a forceful kisser. Instead, he'd been sensitive, curious.

Still, Jamie was superstitious. It had been his first night as a Devil, and he didn't want to break Butler's rules on his very first night. If he got to know Kenny, and knew him outside the bar, then it would be different. But meeting him there and taking him home was strictly against Butler's rules and Jamie didn't want to mess things up.

Kenny was still staring at him. He coughed, regained his composure, and said, "So, coffee then?"

Jamie smiled.

"It's not you. It's the bar. We're not allowed to go home with guys from the bar. If it wasn't my first night, I would break the rules. God, I want to break the rules."

He gave Kenny a serious look. Hoping to convince him that he was telling the truth.

Kenny smiled, but his eyes were distant and serious. "I understand. I know what it's like to mess up a job."

Jamie worried that he'd ruined the mood. "You know what, I still have a ton of adrenaline after all of that. Why don't we walk down to the water? There won't be anyone around. Butler never said anything about *walking* with the guests," he said with a wink.

"That sounds great," Kenny said.

The made their way down Van Ness to Fort Mason and then continued along the water. At first they made small talk. Kenny asked Jamie about the performance, whether or not he'd been nervous, how different it was from go-go dancing. Jamie asked Kenny which of the other dances he'd enjoyed most, about how he'd found Limerick to begin with.

It was still dark as they walked by Crissy Field and toward Fort Point, but the sky was slowly changing from black to grey, and soon the sun would rise.

Jamie felt comfortable and open around Kenny. He didn't reveal much, but he seemed genuinely interested and at ease with Jamie. He was very physical, frequently grabbing Jamie's shoulder or poking his side, which Jamie wouldn't have assumed from looking at him. He looked like the closed-off type.

They by-passed Fort Point and walked south into the Golden Gate National Recreation Area. There was hardly anyone out and about, just a few homeless people and the occasional early morning jogger.

They found a path and walked under the lights, side by side, their shoulders brushing.

Kenny asked, "So, what did you do before you started dancing at Limerick?"

"I don't really want to talk about the past," Jamie said quietly. He felt bad about deflecting but he was having such a good time, and tonight had been such a great night, that he didn't want to descend into disappointment and regret.

He looked over at Kenny, who smiled warmly and said, "You know what, I don't either. But if you don't talk about the past when you're trying to get to know someone, what do you talk about?"

Now Jamie smiled. He thought about it for a second.

"Let's talk about who we're going to be," he said.

*

Kenny walked alongside Jamie, who limped slightly, listening attentively as he described wanting to perform more places, beyond Limerick, maybe even try stage acting.

"But Limerick is so unique," he was saying. "I'd love to stay as long as it's open. That space isn't zoned to be a bar, or a theater, so it won't last forever. They'll have to shut it down. But it rocks. What about you? What's in your future?"

Kenny hadn't thought much about his future. He'd been so concerned about the future he'd imagined for himself, the one he'd messed up, that he'd forgotten to think about the future he wanted.

They walked out onto Baker Beach just as the sun was rising, the sky turning a pure, clean morning blue. The beach was abandoned, and Kenny grabbed Jamie and expertly lowered him to the sand, enveloping him in his arms so that he wouldn't be jarred by the fall.

"I would like my future to involve seeing you naked," he said, smiling wide.

Jamie looked surprised to find himself on the ground so quickly and so firmly wrapped in Kenny's arms. He freed his arms and for a second Kenny worried that he was upset. Then Jamie reached up and grabbed Kenny's face, pulling him into a deep kiss.

When they came up for air, Jamie said, "Well, I promise you can, but tell me what's in your future, first. Tell me something secret." Jamie looked playful, despite the serious question.

Kenny thought about it for a second and then smiled. "I've never told anyone this, at least as an adult, but I love to dance. I'm not nearly as good as you, but I'd love to do it. I used to dance all the time as a kid and I was pretty good at it. Break dancing, hip-hop, that kind of thing. But then life happened and I had to give it up."

Jamie had a look in his eye, like a light bulb had gone off.

"Well," he said, "I might have a proposition for you."

Kenny looked at him, surprised.

"But first, take off your clothes," Jamie said, completely serious.

Kenny looked around. The beach was empty, but soon joggers and tourists would be out.

"You want to do it, here?"

"No, you heathen. Can you imagine all of the places we'd get sand?" Jamie laughed. "But, I promised you could see me naked. But you've got to get naked, too."

Kenny hesitated for a second but then looked at Jamie's beautiful, sharp face, still just inches from his.

"Ah, what the hell."

He reached down and pulled off his shoes. Jamie scooted to the side and watched him. Kenny stood up and took off his T-shirt, slowly, eager to show his body off to Jamie. Jamie watched with obvious interest. Then, he unzipped his jeans and pulled them down with his briefs in one swift move.

Jamie was shameless, staring directly at Kenny's cock. He licked his lips. "Yeah, we'll definitely be seeing each other again. A lot."

Kenny smiled and told him, "your turn."

Jamie stood up, and Kenny noticed that he kept all of his weight on his left leg. He slipped his tank top over his head, and though Kenny had seen his chest at the club, he was still mesmerized by Jamie's long muscles. Jamie slipped off his sneakers and socks and then turned around, his back to Kenny. He pulled his jeans down over his ass slowly, revealing that he wasn't wearing underwear. His ass was glorious, smooth and round, hard and soft. Jamie looked over his shoulder at Kenny and then down at Kenny's rock hard dick.

"Well, I can see that you're interested," Jamie said, smiling.

Kenny stood there, waiting for Jamie to take the lead. Without warning, Jamie ran straight toward the water. The sun was out, and Kenny turned his cap back around to block it before running after Jamie.

He caught up and grabbed Jamie's hand as they ran toward the water. They both leapt as they hit the waves. It was shocking and cold and a complete adrenaline rush. Jamie turned to him and smiled and Kenny smiled back. As the cold water hit his body, Kenny looked north toward the Golden Gate Bridge and felt like he had absolutely no idea what he was doing or where he was headed. And he loved that.

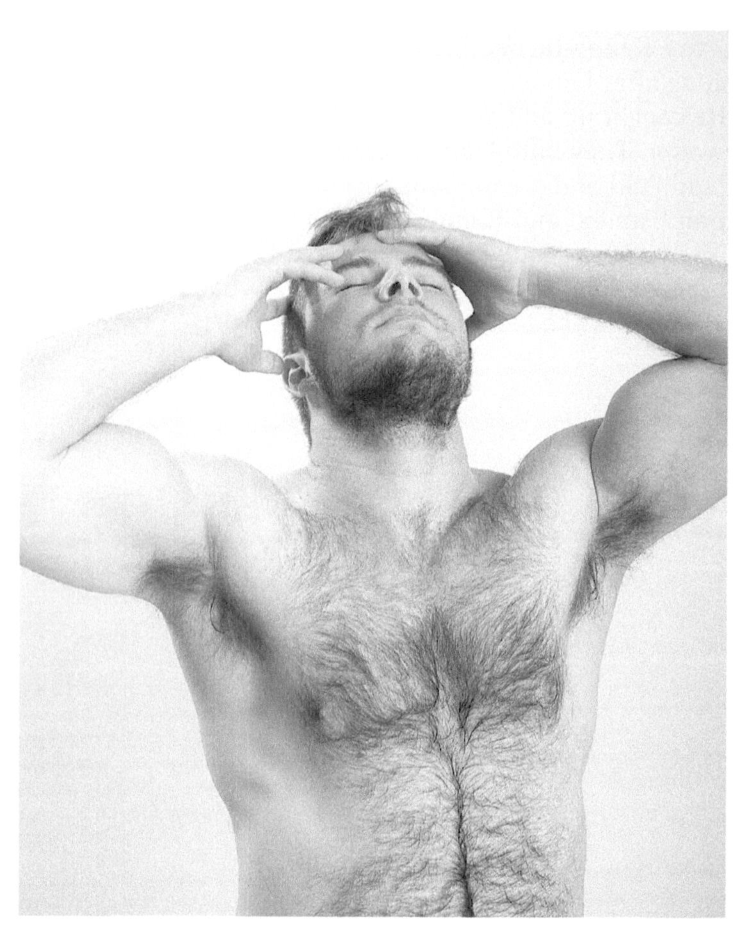

THE TERPSICHOREAN ARTS

Jim Provenzano

You're not you up there, and you know it, so that makes it okay. You're more than just you.

I offer a fiver, since a one's just tacky, and a twenty begs more attention than I'll request from you, because it's not exactly a sex party, but one of those gay Burner Faerie warehouse parties, and people are being all groovy and not into the objectification thing, which I would do, because you seem into it. But the tone of the night is more celebratory than completely seductive.

As I slip the fiver between a strap of your black jock, which is all you're wearing besides boots and a chain necklace, you're perfect. You're a mascot of the evening's erotic game, without need of an animal costume.

I won't do what I want to do, truly fondle your butt cheeks, run my fingers through your perfectly feathered chest hair, because I've met your boyfriend, and I forgot to pop in a breath mint. Plus, you're a bit over lit for such intimate gestures. But don't worry, it's quite flattering.

I could draw your attention down to squatting, giving anyone behind you a marvelous view. I could tell you that I, too, have been up there, thirty years and twenty pounds ago, shaking my ass for tips, because it was fun, and back then I, too, was perfect.

Now, because of those years, I can step outside myself and enjoy viewing the role, the objectified beauty that you've chosen to become tonight.

I could tell you how I once danced atop the bar at Pyramid with Star Booty and two members of the ACT UP Swim Team, but you wouldn't get the references as you had yet to be born, so my retro-bragging will have no effect. Besides, the music just became a bit too loud and techno for a conversation. And besides, I know you're going home to your boyfriend, and this is just a fun gig for you, not an advertisement.

You might be amused by tales of the more interactive fun I've had at official strip joints here and in a few other cities, where, like a fellow fan with whom I've just been chatting, I prefer to sit down front and get there early, to get 'dibs' on the performer's body before it's been slathered over by other patrons.

No, that's not happening tonight, or with you, and that's fine. So I'll merely graze a palm down your thigh, try to vicariously capture the feeling of your movement by touch, which won't work.

Because it's by observing you dance, higher up, admired, that I'm flushed with desire. That is the point. You are a dance floor highlight in Day-Glo yellow marker, an accent of the best of us.

You're a step up from the New Orleans trade I enjoyed last year, but you're not as surprisingly erotic as the Los Angeles muscled stud imported to a San Francisco club, who, after the mere wave of another fiver, grabbed my hand and shoved it into his boxer shorts for more than a few welcome tugs on his erect dick, which thereafter bounced up and down enough to make heads turn.

You're not the long-dead New York porn actor and hustler pal who lured me to The Gaiety for a special backstage body painting session for Halloween weekend, which wowed the other talent so much that I ended up doing the same for astoundingly beautiful young hookers at subsequent parties so long ago.

It was there, before Madonna ruined it all, that I witnessed the myriad ways the hunky talents arouse themselves between the opening teaser dance and the full-boned fully nude strut. That revelation remains a trade secret, except perhaps to you.

You'll never be the surprisingly enthusiastic dancer who, after a few grinding lap dances, gave me his phone number and performed for me in private, by request in my home, before the intense sexual bouts one imagines with a go-go dancer, but rarely experiences. Mine performed for weeks before he found a sugar daddy who could offer more than a few wrinkled dollars and a home-cooked meal.

But you won't go that far. Nope, you're simply dancing casually on a wooden box, and you've already forgotten my name, but who cares, as we're all here at a party to celebrate . . . something.

So I hope you don't mind if I pull back a bit, hang against a wall trying to not look creepy—I forgot your name, too—and just watch you dance.

While once again I'm dancing myself, amid the others, because thankfully the music changed, I may just offer a smiling glance as you thrust and shake your hips, and try to lock a few of those moments into a permanent memory bank.

The monetary transaction is not what makes my admiration honest, or unseemly. It's a frame, a fourth wall of desire. Besides, I only brought enough cash for two more drinks, and I should also be mindful of the less staged flirtation that's happening on the dance floor with an almost equally beautiful man who isn't, that night, a featured act.

You can tell a lot about a man by how he dances. We know you're perfect, with a bit of awkward muscled hunkiness that only endears me more. I notice my dance floor companion admiring you too, and he blushes, and I smile, because I'm not going to explain how you are here to help us feel more sexy.

Because it's working, you sharing your beauty. You being more than you makes us more than ourselves.

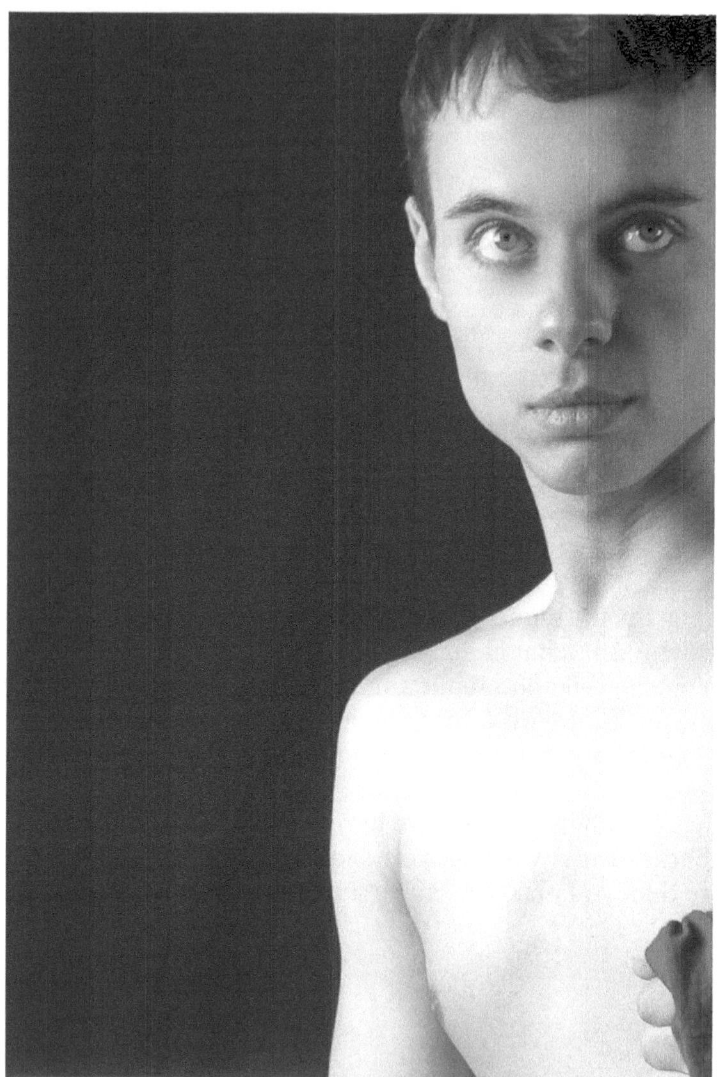

I Am Your Mirror

David Pratt

I don't ask her, "Am I the fairest of them all?" At the door to night, I look into her depths and ask, "Am I enough?"

Lights make the street deeper, the cracked surfaces whole.

I stand in the light. I outshine my blemishes, outshine the stains, if I open myself in just the way they expect at the right moment. Other times, I stand above the crowd and feel queasy because not enough is asked of me, so why am I alive? To fill my stomach, without tragedy or disappointment? To fill my stomach with nothing *but* tragedy and disappointment? "Come, join the fray!" says Lady Vulnerability. No! My coin is that place I hold, above. I can't betray it. I can't start longing to be mortal, like so many before me. I will die, but I pretend otherwise. That is my job.

Men hold out money to me, each paying for his own private reasons, reasons he herds up and takes home with him at the end of the night. Worn, well worked-out but unspoken reasons, old before their time, he gathers and ushers them into the fresh air and light. (The babes should not be allowed in here, poor things!) His reasons for paying me are pampered little hothouse things. Daddy hovers, indulges them, while he pays me and pays me, then leaves me behind in this dim vacuum.

At the height of the height of the evening, in the hooting and the music and the sweat and raised drinks, his reasons for stuffing me with cash bounced up and down and seemed so obvious. His thoughts opened just as I opened, all plain, affable meanings and agreed-upon consequences. I did this, he hooted. I did that, he hollered. I did this, he cheered. I did that, he clapped. But those bouncy reasons were for show. Shiny, temporary things that get accepted as real, night after night, year after year, generation after generation, until they become more real than what is real.

What *is* real?

His *real* reasons for patronizing me—that fragile brood of hideously deformed but perfectly groomed reasons to which he is beholden, though he swears he isn't; that poor brood born with spina bifida or neurofibromatosis—he keeps those reasons from me because I might stick my whatever in them accidentally. I'm allowed to fuck the shiny, fake reasons, but he herds the excuses he cherishes most, the errors he leans on more than he'd ever lean on me, more than he'd lean on just the idea of me (which breaks and gives way so easily)—he herds those tidy grotesques to the door and chauffeurs them home, where blankies swaddle them, where choo-choos smile, and plush piggies snuggle.

I count up how much I was given tonight to feed those cherished ones I may not touch, while my own brood is left thin, stunted, half-dressed, sobbing in the glow of an empty refrigerator.

He is married to the painted queen they call Lady Vulnerability. Together they have borne these larval self-arguments, twisted or with their organs on the outside. The marriage has not worked out—the horrid larvae are the evidence—but he will never leave Lady V.

He could buy me for the whole night, give me all his cash, I'd cuddle and coo and feed, but he'd go home to the arms of Lady V. And I'd return home and ask, "Mirror, mirror on the wall—why am I not enough?"

She doesn't answer. I, too, have slept with Lady Vulnerability. We produced our brood, baby birds gaping, tiny, soft, quivering engines of want, little hard-ons or huge sperm cells, wanting to make make make, having to feed feed feed, shit shit shit.

Now she speaks, my mirror. "You have killed them."

"Killed? Who? I soothe them. I distract them. How could I kill them?"

"Not the men. They stay on life support stuffing your jock."

"Then who?" The sun is burning already, the outside humid and lifeless. Not like the night.

"Their little ones. Their broods of reasons, arguments and suppositions."

Oh, them.

"The stories they tell themselves. With a perfect twist of your hip, you undo them. That drum of skin below your sternum, trembling, undermines them, infects them, disintegrates them. Flutter your lashes from Nowheresville, USA, and you kill their theories. Your supposed beauty and independence might strengthen some reasons, might fortify certain tales and excuses for a moment no one can even identify. But the tip of your tongue across your lower lip kills others. Instantly their dads seize them and try to resuscitate them. They're trying now, in the gray-yellow dawn, behind the chophouse. But as the Sun burns they see their tales are truly dead. They bring the corpses to your feet, to see if the same eyes that killed them last night will resuscitate them tonight. You will bend and part your lips, but you will only kill more. You will put to rest the thought that their daddies might be young again, that they might wake in a timeless place across the ocean, that all they once let slip might still be as available to them as you are. They won't bury their dead stories. They will keep hoping, keep bringing your victims back to you. They stink, but the men don't smell them. And you just kill more."

"I don't mean to! I am innocent!" I do those things to keep myself alive. And yes, they are failing, but I believed myself to be the only one hurt.

"That is why I am offering you an easy penance."

"Penance?"

"Seven years. With us. Seven years as a mirror. It's steady work, and you're good at reflecting, returning light, answering the desperate flicker from the middle of the ocean. Come. We accept you. One of us."

"No, please!" I step back. Still she reflects me, returns my poor light perfectly to me.

"Without us, some don't know they exist. They keep checking; we confirm, accurately. They are the only ones who lie. Come. We accept you. One of us."

My body. Open to all men, so long as I reflect their dreams and don't reflect time. But that's impossible. Try thinking about time for one second, without thinking about its end. Time, father of all endings. There are no windows where I dance. No clocks. Music that never repeats so you never think, *Didn't I hear that a poor hour ago*?

You can fight time, kill yourself slowly with yet another dollar in my jock. Kill yourself quickly, get revenge on time. But time can't stop, either. It is addicted to itself.

That man—his deformed little stories are raised as anti-timers. To each thought doodad he ties a ribbon: "Time does not exist." Bring him before me. In all my attempts to erase time I will provide him with devastating evidence of its existence. I suggest a narrative, The One Great Narrative from which my observer is excluded, and all his carefully constructed fantasies are dying off.

"It's steady work, this perfect reflecting, this truth-telling, this hanging from the wall. We accept you, one of us."

Until now, the men and I confirmed each other's existence. I tell the truth, only the truth. They lie. They defy time's declaration, "You are nothing," the same thing their mothers and fathers told them. Until now, the men filled the emptiness with dollars, stuffed in my jock. I filled the same emptiness with my bare and barely blemished body, withheld at the last second. But their dollars are play money, my jock, a costume, a form of armor, fetishized, lying. Armored in my jock, concealing, revealing, I made the men believe that I—or someone, at least—would always be there, that they could possess forever what cannot be touched or seen or even named.

They can possess such a thing. But not with my jock as intermediary.

"We accept you. Seven years."

Here in my cubicle, I produce. In narrow hallways I deliver. The building breathes. If I don't produce, it will shit me out and eat someone else. Always someone else in this city. Make someone need you and they won't let you go. Because their squalling brood of arguments bawls for your execution.

I can't babysit excuses forever. Reflecting is steady work, no risk. The need for reflection never runs out. I feel secure, even superior: still at last, but still moving; securely owned but independent in thought; false (aren't we all?), but true to things I think I believe. Bring me a young man. He will ask if he is enough, and he will be mine. The world belongs to mirrors. He will be at my mercy. I will not be happy or beloved. I will not love. But I will keep my power.

I just wonder if, at the end of it all, my men will still want me. The infinite longing in their eyes was nice. The sigh in their voices. The supposition that, for a second, I completed them. That was nice. And the supposition that I and what I did were worth money, the ultimate form of self-expression. Getting that was the nicest of all. Having it meant little. Losing it makes me free.

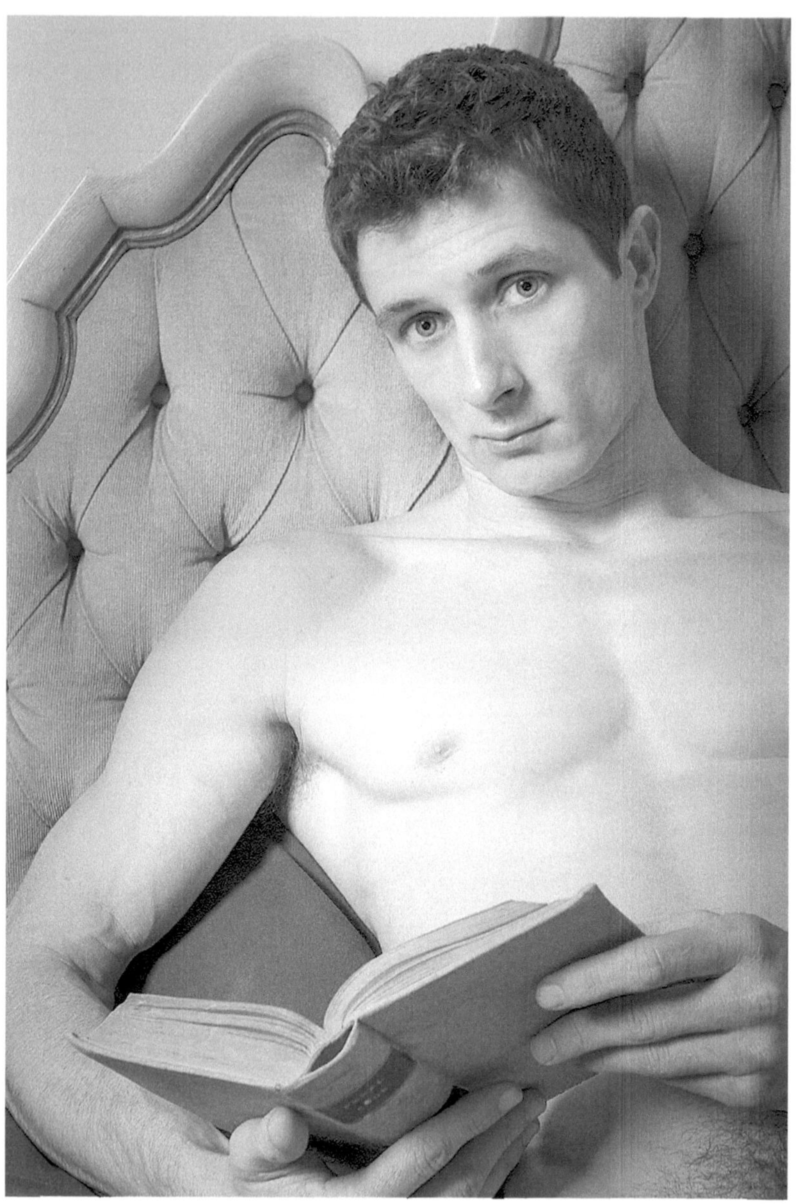

Falling like Icarus

Stephen Mead

His eyes look up
from the book, green-grey,
a certain shade of agate when wet
in a melt of clarity
somehow both direct and searching.

There seems to be no preoccupation left
for the yellowed red leather-bound pages
soft for his elegant hands
of tapered gentleness.

In this there is mesmerism,
those fingers capable of holding,
caressing skin as deftly
as though cradling the head of a lover.

Imagine being so close to the silk radiance
of his bare, hairless chest,
its Singer-Sergeant slopes and flats
the classical collar bones, the nipples, roseate.

Imagine being held against such Renaissance youth
brought back in living flesh
with a velvet headboard of saffron yellow
supporting the combined strength
where kindness meets desire.

Reflective, his focus holds all that and more,
or so a lonesome soul hopes, projects perhaps,

holding nothing back to protect
something for himself
from this promise of beauty
at last spirit-deep.

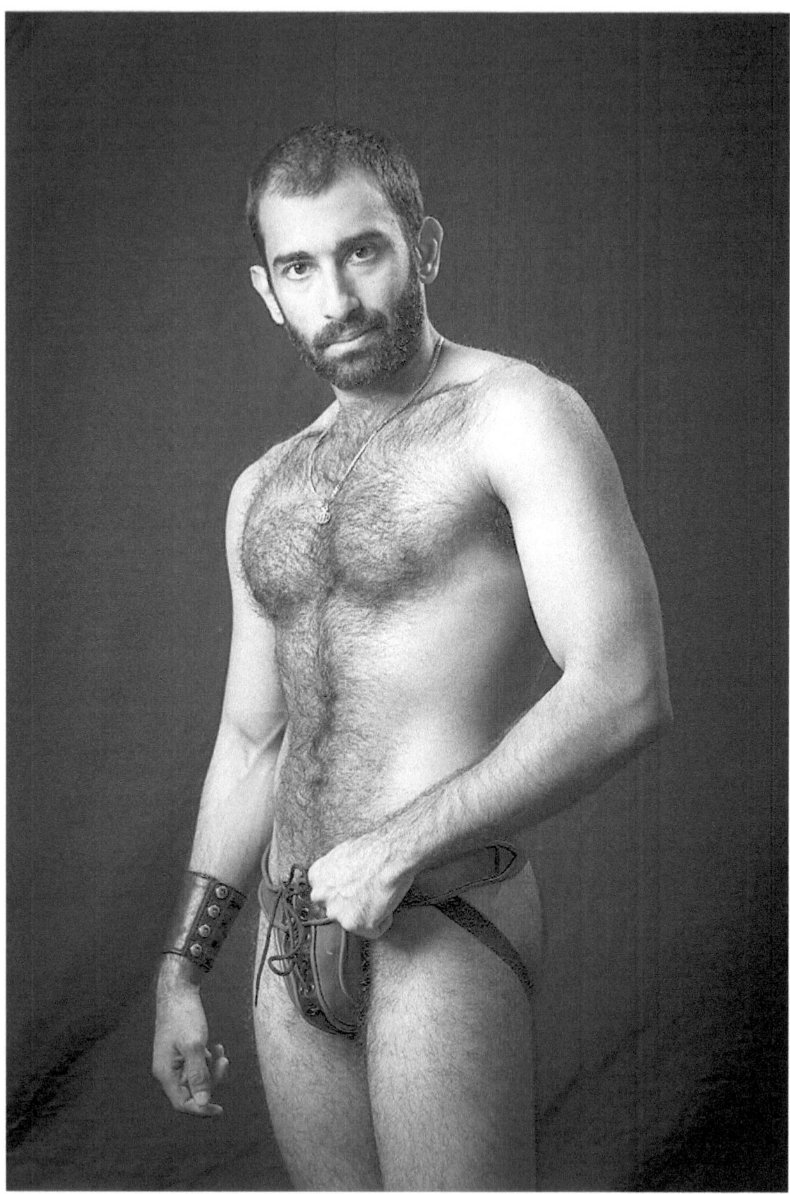

Hypothetically
Jeff Mann

Let's say I'm single, at least for the night.
Let's say, having escaped the tedium
of some academic conference, I'm sipping peaty
Scotch in a gay go-go club and watching
a dark-eyed, dark-bearded boy lithely
dance in nothing but a silver chain, a black
leather wristband, and a black and blue
lace-up jockstrap. He's
as furry as all my Muses, with pecs well-
defined and thick-pelted, arms lightly
muscled, flat belly lean with youth.
His intense features evoke the Middle East,
and the black leather about his wrist seems
to bespeak the kink I crave. See how
my starved-bear stare and offerings of money
snare his focus, how with larger and larger
denominations I plead for much more
than this erect moment's maddening mere visual.
See how I ache for touch, a sweaty scene
together, however costly and evanescent.
When at last I beckon, he leans nearer—
solemn glance, enflaming scent of musk—
and so I ask, "Are you for hire?" and so
he nods, and so I ask, "How much
for kink and an overnight? I've never paid
before," and so he rasps a number inside
music's boom and manic stutter. See
how simply frustration's finished and the likelihood
of satiation swells? In my hotel, I strip

us both, I kiss him hard, I tie his hands
behind his back. The helpless way he leans
against me, the way he calls me "Daddy," lapping
my silver-streaked goatee and hardening so fast
inside my grip are raptures well worth
both price and wait. Now I bind his feet,
ease him onto the bed, gently chew
his nipples, stroke his hairy thighs, fondle
the fur in the crack of his ass. "Is this your world?"
he sighs, just before I push a rag
between his teeth and knot it behind his head.
"Yes," I say, squeezing his biceps, kneading
his hirsute pecs, reaching for the lube.
"This is the rich world I make with words,
narrow but most accommodating," I say,
giving his ass cheeks a series of slaps, "a jagged
column of rhythmic black letters poured over
a white page," pushing a greased finger
inside him, making him whimper, "white as empty
as the space between stars, emptiness stolid
and sad as most facts and many lives,"
bending his supple form double, watching
his black eyes widen, his white teeth
gnash the gag, as I slip stiff flesh
inside him and begin the immemorial thrusting,
sighing, riding, rocking. Here are imagination's
miracles, reality's infinite alternatives,
born of the photo of a beautiful bearded stranger—
the Platonic Form of male perfection and surrender
grunting and bucking beneath me, the dark god

my moist and happy sacrifice, ass-ravished
raw, held bound and gagged all the naked
night, nestled warm and snoring in my arms.

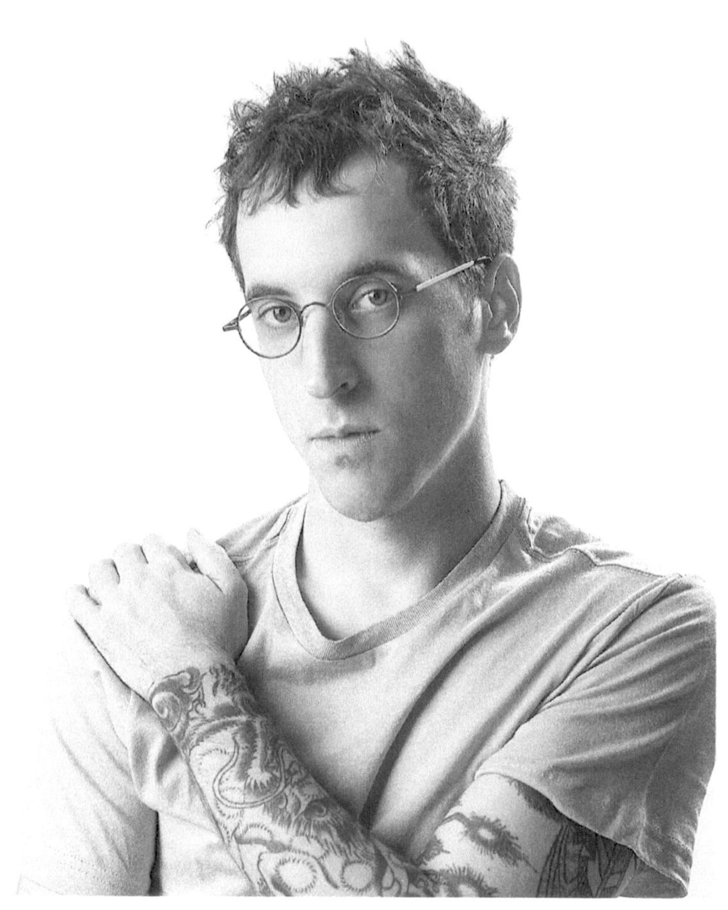

Bound

'Nathan Burgoine

Matthew had three problems: his inheritance was getting stronger, his great-grandfather was suspicious, and he'd forgotten the name of the naked werewolf beside him. Only one of these problems had an immediate solution at hand.

James? Jason? Something with a J. *Damn.*

He craned his neck, grateful there was no hangover, though he felt fuzzy enough to know he'd enjoyed more drink than strictly smart. The man in bed with him was on his back and—if Matthew was honest with himself—a welcome sight.

Matthew himself was lean and trim. He loved to swim and run, activities that let him outpace his thoughts and intuitions, and those preferences telegraphed themselves in his body. The man beside him was built thicker, with wide shoulders, strong arms, and a chest with a deep cleft between the muscles. Where Matthew often felt too clean-cut, the man was instead all rough edges.

Matthew took a slow breath and called his magic to the surface. Never difficult—especially over the last year or so, with the inheritance making itself known—it thrummed in his blood, an eager tide of power.

Reaching into the air between them, Matthew cupped his hand as though trying to catch pouring water. He replayed the memory of their meeting in the dive bar where he'd finally parked his motorcycle after hours of riding.

The magic swirled in his cupped palm.

Hi, Matthew remembered himself saying. *I'm Matt.*

Matthew tipped his hand, and let the magic pull him. He slipped past their introductions, tasted beer, heard the man's low, rumbling voice, and remembered laughing, dancing with him, and an offer to head back to his place eagerly received. The images blurred—sensations of hairy skin and sweat—and then a blissful night of sleep not haunted by his growing gift. To now, where he felt an echo of himself from moments before, beginning the spell and calling back to the memory . . .

And then past. Into an ephemeral conversation moments from now. The world grew foggy, and it was hard to focus on more than one thing at a time.

"Good morning," the man would say, when he opened his eyes and saw Matthew was already awake.

"Can I just admit I don't remember your name?" Matthew's voice was distorted in his own ears, the conversation that hadn't yet occurred coming to him as though from the other end of a tunnel.

"It's fine. We were a little busy with other things." Matthew liked this man's voice, even as warped by magic as it was. "It's Jace. And you're Matt, right?"

Matt closed his hand. The magic broke across his skin, drifting up his arm and seeping back inside him.

Beside him, the man opened his eyes.

"Good morning," he said, smiling when he saw Matthew looking down at him.

"Hi," Matthew said.

"Do you always watch guys sleep?" the man asked. His shoulders cracked as he stretched his arms over his head, and Matthew's eyes were drawn to the muscle beneath the dark hair that covered his forearms and the lines of ink that wrapped around the biceps on his left arm, a chain of phases of the moon done in an intricate spiral.

"Only when they're hot," Matthew said.

The man's smile was wicked. "You hoping for a morning tussle?"

"Actually, I was hoping you would join me in the shower, and maybe give me a ride back to the bar. My motorcycle's there."

Jace's grin widened. He rolled, pinning Matthew's shoulders and sliding on top of him. His weight felt good there, and there was little doubt that if Matthew wanted a morning "tussle," Jace was up for it.

"So you're at my mercy."

Matthew's resolve slipped at the heat in the man's dark eyes.

"A little bit," he said.

"And here I thought you were just slumming out of view of your family."

That was a bit too on the mark for comfort, but with the weight of the man—and an eager hardness—on him, Matthew couldn't begrudge the impression.

"I'm not slumming." Matthew lifted his head to catch a kiss. "Though it's true what they say about werewolves."

Jace's eyes widened, and Matthew grinned. "What? I'm not supposed to know?"

He inhaled deeply. "You're not a were," Jace said, zero doubt in his voice.

"Mage," Matthew said. "A wizard."

Jace eyed him. "You didn't mention that last night."

"You didn't tell me you were a werewolf last night."

The sly grin slowly returned. "Fair enough." Jace leaned down and rubbed his stubble along Matthew's neck. Matthew felt his back arch, more of his resolve to get on the road fading under friction. He moaned.

"So," Jace whispered close in Matthew's ear. "What *do* they say about werewolves?"

"Animal in the streets, beast in the sheets," Matthew said.

Jace laughed. Matthew ran his hands across the man's thick, hairy chest and the last of his resolve faded. Jace lowered himself down on top of him and the two kissed again, a long, heated kiss that made it perfectly clear neither was going to suggest a shower or anything else soon.

Jace broke off. "What about wizards?"

"Pardon?" Matthew said, breathless.

"What do they say about wizards?"

"Oh," Matthew said. "We're just magic."

Jace's smirk struck Matthew as a challenge. He willed magic to the surface and let it spread, the heat pulsing between them with a warmth like stepping into a hot bath. The slight aches of the night before were soothed, and hot, swirling caresses looped around their bodies, feeling like hands, tongues, and mouths.

Jace arched his neck, gasping at the sudden onslaught of sensations.

"See? Magic."

After that, they didn't talk at all.

*

Rain made the ride home a misery. Matthew parked the bike in the garage, his shoulders aching from the tension. He put his helmet on the bike, then tugged down the zipper of his jacket. His jeans were soaked, and he wanted nothing more than a long hot bath.

Walking into the house, however, he realized that wasn't going to happen.

His father and great-grandfather were both waiting for him.

"Where have you been?"

His great-grandfather, of course. No one spoke before Malcolm Stirling, not even a father to his son. The words themselves lacked any apparent disapproval, but Matthew knew better. He glanced at his father, who refused to meet his gaze. There would be no help from that quarter.

Matthew took a deep breath. He needs you. There's only so much they can do to you. Don't let him rattle you.

"I went for a ride."

"In the rain?" From another, it might have sounded like concern. Malcolm Stirling was not a tall man and nearly eighty, but there was nothing soft about him. Even on Saturday he was dressed in a tailored suit, complete with his signature navy blue tie. His cane—which might have made another man seem vulnerable—instead granted him even more authority, as though it were a judge's gavel.

Or an executioner's axe. Matthew knew it was heavily enchanted.

"I was out overnight." He took satisfaction in the smallest widening of Malcolm's eyes.

"Overnight," Malcolm repeated.

Icy nervousness spread through him. He swallowed. "I'm wet and cold. Could I dry off, maybe?"

The moment the words were out of his mouth, he knew it was a mistake. He forced a neutral expression, hiding the flinch when Malcolm's countenance darkened.

"Young man, do not speak to me in that manner."

Matthew waited. Nothing he said would help at this point. His magic roiled under his skin. He tried to calm down, working hard to appear unaffected.

"Where did you go?" Malcolm said, after a moment.

"I visited a friend." Happily, there was no truth spell in effect, as Matthew had zero doubt that calling Jace a friend would have tipped an enchanted feather off its tip. There was no way he'd explain a vision-induced werewolf one-night stand to his great-grandfather.

"Do we know this friend?" Malcolm asked.

"No," Matthew said. "He's new." Inspiration struck. "I thought it had something to do with my gift." He spoke in a rush, hoping to sound embarrassed. It wasn't far from true.

Malcolm swallowed. "Explain."

Shit. "I saw him in some dreams, so . . ." Matthew shrugged, hoping it made sense he'd race to a friend after dreaming about him. He didn't bother explaining it had been weeks, or that he'd never met this "friend" before, or that in dreams, this "friend" was never wearing clothes, though he had some beautiful tattoo work. "I thought maybe . . ." He let his voice trail off.

"You need to bind your gift," Malcolm said. A familiar refrain. "You need a tool you control to take charge of the sight."

You mean pick Tarot or runes or something you can ask me to do so you can stay top dog in the Families, like when you had prescience, and when your son did, and when my father did.

"I know," Matthew said. "I can't find the right tool."

A line formed between Malcolm Stirling's eyebrows. "The runes didn't work?"

Matthew exhaled. "*Everything* works, but it's not under control." He looked at his father when he said this, and for the briefest moment, he felt his father's support. They had the same eyes—and the same nearsightedness—and the compassion that shone in his father's gaze might have been brief, but it gave him some confidence that he could still find a way out from under his great-grandfather's thumb.

He wouldn't be the family oracle if he could help it.

"There are nearly endless ways of measuring the future," Malcolm said.

"Well, I sure don't want to read entrails," Matthew said, but he said it with enough of a smile it sounded like a joke.

"Certainly not." Malcolm's lips offered the briefest echo of a smile.

"Go have a bath," his father said. Matthew was surprised his father was giving him the out, but Malcolm didn't seem upset. "We can talk later. There's a meeting soon, and you're not presentable."

Ah. That made sense. Heaven forbid the other coven heads see me in wet jeans.

Matthew took the excuse to leave, grateful for the exit.

*

After a bath, Matthew ditched gritty contacts for his glasses. In dry clothes he snuck down to the ground floor and past the closed doors of the study. He heard the muffled voices of the coven heads inside—four men, one woman. The last thing he wanted was to be around when they finished. In deference to his great-grandfather's penchant for looking "suitable," he wore dress pants and a crisp, long-sleeved white collared shirt.

He slipped from the kitchen into the large yard. The rain had stopped, and though the sun was barely breaking through, it was warm. He made his way to the gazebo across wet grass. With every step, pressure released from his shoulders.

On the threshold of the gazebo, he saw it was already occupied. A broad smile—the first since he'd woken up this morning beside Jace—broke across Matthew's face.

"Hi," Mackenzie Windsor said.

She was the daughter of Katrina Windsor, the only woman to hold a position of coven head in the Families of Ottawa. Katrina was new to the role, Mackenzie's grandfather having passed at the start of summer. They'd known each other since they were kids, when the comings and goings of their parents hadn't made sense, before they'd come into their own magic and learned who they were. Mackenzie wore a green dress and dark brown shawl, and her hair—usually a curling mess that she wore tied back—was instead bound with two chopsticks and a ribbon, a single curled ringlet left to hang beside her cheek.

"Kenzie? In a dress? It can't be."

"Laugh it up, nerd. Nice shirt."

"They made you dress up?" Matthew said.

"I wasn't even allowed to wear my boots," Mackenzie said, pointing at a pair of moderately-heeled black pumps. Her feet were bare. "Those things are torture."

Matthew sat beside her. "Any idea what they're talking about?"

"Something new," Mackenzie said. "Apparently there's an orphan out there forming his own coven."

Matthew leaned back. "Can he do that?" He wondered if that could be a way to get away from his great-grandfather, but dismissed it. Even in another coven, he'd still *be* Matthew Stirling. As long as he had a pipeline into the future, there was no way Malcolm would let him be beholden to anyone but Malcolm.

"I think that's what the meeting is about. I didn't get all the details," Mackenzie said. "I don't know if there's other orphans around. He'd need two more, right?"

"It takes three," Matthew said. Three wizards for a coven. Three vampires for a coterie. Three demons or weres for a pack.

Speaking of which.

"So, it's getting worse," Matthew said.

Mackenzie pulled her legs up underneath her and leaned her head on his shoulder. "Your dreams?"

"Yep," he said. "I wish I'd kept the receipt, because I'd like to return this gift and exchange it for something else."

"I'm sure your father would, too."

Matthew snorted. That was true. His father had relished being Malcolm's seer. Reading runes for Malcolm, divining the future—all of it gave his father purpose. Then his readings had stopped being reliable, and Matthew started having dreams about things that hadn't yet happened. It became clear the Stirling gift had moved on.

It wasn't fair. His father hadn't gotten the gift from Matthew's grandfather until he was in his thirties. Matthew was barely twenty.

"Malcolm's really on my case to bind it." His voice shook.

"Of course he is," Mackenzie said. "He's used to having access. When your father used the runes, Malcolm could watch every stone he pulled. He might not have divined the nuances that your father could, but he could certainly follow. Anyone can, if they know the meanings. You said he used runes too, when he had the gift, right?"

"Yeah. And my grandfather used Tarot."

"Malcolm wants something he can understand, so he's not at your mercy. He wants control." She wasn't speaking unkindly, and he knew she was sympathetic, but it still felt bleak. "We need an option he can't read over your shoulder."

"I tried scrying with a bowl—I'm so keyed in to water as an element I thought it might work—but it was random information, not what I asked. Just like the dreams." Matthew exhaled. "And you know what Malcolm would say, 'Dreaming is not a suitable outlet, Matthew. It's not masterable. The gift must be bound to a tool, something solid, something available when you desire it.'"

"Something I can use to my advantage," Mackenzie said, mimicking his great-grandfather's officious and emotionless tone.

Matthew smiled. "Yep. That."

They sat quietly for a while.

"What if you don't?" Mackenzie asked.

"Pardon?"

"If you don't bind it. What happens?"

"The dreams get stronger. I'll have visions when I'm awake, and . . ." He exhaled. "Ever heard of the Oracles?"

"As in the Greek Oracles?"

"Yep. Crazy lunatics spouting off prophecies and living in sealed caves."

"Ah," Mackenzie said. "So, not that."

"Not that. Though I took a four hour motorcycle ride to meet someone I've been dreaming about for weeks," Matthew said. "Which is crazy enough."

Mackenzie leaned away. "Seriously?"

Matthew nodded, closing his eyes. "Yep. Every time I try to ask the gift for a way to bind it that doesn't lead to me trapped, I see this guy." Even as he was saying the words, Jace was coming to his mind. His wide shoulders, broad chest, dark eyes, the tattoo chain of the phases of the moon. Over and over, he'd seen that tattoo, that arm, the man's strong, masculine body. It had finally driven him to scrying. He'd spent four hours looping around when he'd feel his intuition telling him he'd gone too far, or needed to head west. The trip home had been less than an hour and a half.

"Who is he?"

"Some random werewolf," Matthew said. He opened his eyes. Mackenzie had one eyebrow raised.

"Some random werewolf," she repeated.

Matthew shrugged. "He has a pack. He's not a lone wolf. He's not the leader. He's twenty-seven. He's a mechanic. He's–"

"Cute?" Mackenzie said.

Matthew blushed. "It's possible he's attractive."

"Well, don't let him bite." Mackenzie shoved his shoulder. Then she stopped, and went a little pale. "It wouldn't be that, would it? Like how most wizards lose their magic if they become a vampire?"

Matthew shook his head. "A bite from a werewolf in wolf form usually kills. But as far as I can tell from lore, *if* I survived I'd have all the same magic I already had, only hairier."

Mackenzie seemed shaken. "You considered it."

Matthew shrugged.

"We'll figure something out. Your element is water. There has to be some form of divination we're missing tied to water, or other liquid, or maybe moonstone?" She sighed. "Something."

"Water isn't good at being bound. All my magic is better when I let it flow free and find its own way. It might be hopeless." Matthew leaned back on the wooden bench. Not for the first time, he envied Kenzie's alignment with earth magic. Earth was—literally—grounded. "Maybe I need to suck it up. Use runes. I mean, how long can the man live?"

"Out of spite? At least a hundred," Mackenzie said.

Matthew laughed, but it wasn't funny.

*

"You need to understand something."

Matthew started. He'd been lying on his bed since the coven heads had left and hadn't heard his great-grandfather approach, nor his door open. He sat up, then rose, not wanting to be on his back while Malcolm Stirling was nearby.

"Okay," Matthew said.

"The Stirling gift of prophecy has been used for generations for us to learn about the people who surround us: whom to trust, who has the best interests of others at heart." Each word was spoken softly, but they still sounded like a threat. Malcolm stared at Matthew, both hands resting on the top of his cane. "Everything we've earned as one of the Families can be traced back to that powerful gift, Matthew. Now it's yours. Yours to use for the good of the family."

Matthew felt sick.

"You need to bind it," Malcolm said. "Or it will rule you."

"Believe me," Matthew said. "I get that."

Malcolm's eyes narrowed. "Try the runes again." He slipped one hand into his suit pocket and pulled out a grey silk pouch and tossed it onto Matthew's bed. "See what they counsel you."

Matthew swallowed. "I'll try."

"Good." Malcolm turned to go, but hesitated at the last moment, one hand on Matthew's door. "Don't chase dreams, Matthew."

Matthew blinked.

"Dreams can become nightmares."

Malcolm closed the door. A moment later, Matthew heard his great-grandfather's voice and the man's magic pulsed through the door. There was an audible click.

Malcolm had locked him in and ensorcelled the door. Matthew sank onto his bed, breathing heavily. He closed his eyes. *Please, please, please . . .*

Tanned skin. A muscled, hairy chest. A strong jaw. Arms lined with veins over muscle, and decorated with moons in a chain . . .

Matthew opened his eyes, grabbed his keys off the dresser, and opened his window.

*

"Hi."

If Jace was surprised to see Matthew on his doorstep, it didn't show. It looked like he hadn't been home long, judging from the once-blue shirt that was now covered in grease stains and the matching dirty jeans.

"Nice glasses," Jace said. He stepped aside and gestured for Matthew to come in.

"Thanks." Matthew stepped in. "I need your help."

Jace looked wary. "What do you mean?"

"I honestly don't know."

Jace frowned. "What?"

"I'm prescient," Matthew said.

Jace's frown grew. "Sorry?"

"I see the future," Matthew said. "That's the problem. I'm . . . important to someone in the Families, and he wants me to use my gift to his advantage, which is what's been done for generations. I don't want to. He's not a good man."

"We wolves know about the Families," Jace said. "But what's it to do with me? You flicks don't like wolves . . . well, usually." His smile made Matthew think about their "tussle." He blushed.

"Every time I look into my future to find a way out, I see you."

"Me," Jace said.

"You," Matthew said.

"Just . . . me," Jace said. "I'm flattered."

"Just you." Matthew sighed with frustration. "No clothes, even."

"I was naked?" The smile was back.

"Yep."

"So you tracked me down and seduced me, just to get me naked?" Jace was moving past amusement and into cocky now.

"That's overstating," Matthew said.

"I'd wondered why a cute thing like you was so itchy." At Matthew's expression, Jace raised his hands. "Hey, I'm not complaining. I was happy to scratch. You didn't need magic to get me. I'm happy to strip if you are." Jace took a step toward him.

"Look, I'm really in trouble here," Matthew said. "I didn't come for sex."

"What did you come for?" Jace reached out and took him by the waist. Matthew didn't resist.

"I don't know," Matthew said. "Another look, I think. I hope seeing you will trigger more visions, show me the way out from under my great-grandfather's control . . ."

"You want me naked," Jace's grin was toothy, "because you hope it will give you a vision? I have to say, Matt, that's probably the best come-on line ever."

"It's not a come-on."

"That's why it's hot."

"Maybe this was a mistake," Matthew said.

"Hey," Jace said, his voice gentle now. "Sorry. I can be an ass sometimes. You appeal to my animal side, and he's not subtle. If I can help, I'll help. You seem like a good guy. Also, you've got the nicest little ass."

"Gee, thanks."

"Seriously edible."

"Shut up and take your clothes off."

Jace winked, took a step back, and pulled off his shirt.

Matthew let the magic rise. He didn't guide, didn't ask, he just let it flow however it wanted to. His gaze trailed across Jace's chest, thick with muscle and covered with wonderful dark hair, then the man's flat stomach, and then up to his shoulders, and down his strong arms and the intricate moon tattoo surrounding the man's biceps . . .

A shock lanced up Matthew's back.

"Matt?" Jace's voice sounded far away.

Like a wave crashing over him, Matthew was lost in the vision.

They were in Ottawa. He could hear chimes from the Peace Tower. Indoors, with light daylight coming in through windows. Buzzing. A slight pain, like a cat's scratch. He was sitting. Jace was beside him, one hand on Matthew's shoulder. Across from them, someone else. Matthew was leaning oddly—where was he? Why was his arm stretched out, and what was the third man doing? The pain—that irritating scratch—continued. Matthew looked down, through the foggy disorientation of the vision and saw lines on his arm. Lines drawn in ink.

Ink.

Matthew stumbled back, and if Jace hadn't moved to catch him, he would have fallen over the back of the small table by the door.

"Hey," Jace said. "Matt. Come back."

Matthew blinked a few times. He looked down at the arms steadying him, and smiled.

"Who did your tattoo?"

Jace let go of Matthew slowly, as though he wasn't sure that Matthew still might not topple over. "My friend Zack. He's a wolf, like me."

"He has a place in Ottawa, right?"

"In the Market," Jace said. "Why?"

"I don't suppose he allows walk-ins?"

Jace regarded him for a long moment. "Does this mean you don't want me to take off my pants?"

*

Matthew expected Zack to be a big burly biker type, but instead he was as lean as Matthew himself, had long blond hair tied back in a man-bun, and the softest voice Matthew had ever heard. He was as unthreatening a man as Matthew had ever met. Even the tattoos that covered both of Zack's forearms to the wrists were almost all cartoons. There was even a Smurf.

He didn't look like a werewolf.

When Matthew explained what he wanted, Zack said he could squeeze him in, and had gone to make a template. Matthew wasn't sure what that meant, but Zack returned with a piece of paper with the pattern printed on it, which would transfer to his skin for Zack to trace.

He pressed it against Matthew's forearm.

Jace growled.

"What's wrong?" Matthew asked. The look on Jace's face was aggressive and none too pleasant.

"It's because I'm marking you," Zack said.

Jace let out a little grunt.

"And?" Matthew said, looking between them.

"It bothers his wolf," Zack said. He smiled at Matthew, and Matthew realized Zack was purposefully not looking at Jace. "Though his wolf knows full well I prefer ladies."

Matthew glanced at Jace. "Really?"

"It's fine," Jace said, but Matthew could tell he was trying to sound casual.

"Wolves are territorial," Zack said. "Me inking you is like I'm touching his property."

"Is that supposed to be flattering?" Matthew asked. "Because it's not."

"Take it as a compliment. You ready?" Zack lifted the template, and there was the simple triangle on his skin, waiting for the tattoo needle. Zack reached behind him, and the machine buzzed.

"Yep," Matthew said.

"And you're sure all you want is a triangle?"

"It's a symbol for water," Matthew said. "Water's my element." He met Zack's gaze. "If anything unusual happens, I just need you to keep going, okay?"

Zack frowned. "What does that mean?"

"No idea. I'm letting the magic lead. Go with the flow. Finish the triangle, ignore anything else."

"Flicks," Zack muttered, but he nodded.

Matthew looked down at the triangle. He took a deep breath, and drew the magic as far to the surface as he dared, feeling it swirling and frothing beneath his skin. His vision grew cloudy around the edges, and then a warm hand settled on his shoulder. Jace.

"Okay," Matthew said.

When the needle touched his skin Matthew let the magic loose. Water was his element. Water. Blood.

Ink.

I bind you, Matthew thought, and when Jace squeezed his shoulder, he realized he'd said the words aloud.

Zack began the first line, calm and assured with the needle, and Matthew barely felt the scratching sensation above the roar filling his ears. The magic wanted out, always had, and now he'd offered it a place to go. As Zack reached the first point of the triangle, the power leapt, finding the ink and the blood and reaching closer to the surface than ever before.

Spirals branched away from the black line of ink Zack drew. Curves and curls forming single waves, then whole rivers. The lines spread from Zack's needle, and across Matthew's forearm, moving before their eyes.

"Jesus," Zack said, but didn't falter.

"I bind you," Matthew said. For the first time in months, he felt something new.

Control.

"I bind you."

Zack began the second line of the triangle, and once again the ink spread toward Matthew's wrist, scales and fish and images of creatures real and fantastical.

"I bind you."

The last line birthed mists and rain that climbed to the crook of Matthew's elbow.

As Zack closed off the triangle, the three lines forming one single shape, Matthew spoke once more.

"You are bound."

The patterns of ink withdrew, twining in and over themselves and pulling back across his skin like things alive, until nothing remained but the simple triangle of black ink.

Zack sat back in his seat. "Damn wizards."

Jace squeezed his shoulder.

Matthew smiled.

*

"You live here?" Jace looked at the huge house.

"It's been in the family a long time," Matthew said. He felt a kind of shame over the opulence, but a single night in Jace's small and tidy house had felt more comforting than any time in Stirling Manor.

Jace stuffed his hands into his pockets. He'd gotten out of his truck when Matthew pulled his motorcycle to the side of the road. Matthew wasn't ready to go inside yet.

"So," Jace said. "I guess that's it, huh?" He looked at Matthew's forearm, where the triangle was visible. He hadn't needed a bandage. Binding the power had healed it.

"I hope so," Matthew said.

"I guess I wasn't your fate."

Matthew blinked. "What?"

Jace's grin was charming. "It was pretty cool. You had visions about me. I guess I got it in my head that maybe I was . . . I don't know. Something." He blushed. "I guess I was just a roadmap. This way to Zack." He pointed.

"You don't get it," Matthew said.

Jace tilted his head.

"It was never about finding my fate," Matthew said. "It was about me having a future."

Jace smiled.

"And besides, your wolf claimed me as property, no?"

Jace reached forward and tugged Matthew closer. "Wolves can be possessive that way. Still, it was pretty nice thinking you couldn't close your eyes without seeing me naked."

Matthew leaned forward. "I'm still gonna do that."

Jace laughed.

Matthew kissed him. It was a light kiss, but there was promise in it.

"You have my number," Jace said. "Use it."

"I will."

*

"I'm back."

Both his great-grandfather and his father were in the study, papers spread before them. They rose as one.

"You can't keep running off, son," his father spoke, surprising Matthew. He wondered if Malcolm had supplied his father with exactly what words to use. "I know this is overwhelming, but you have to control it or it will control you."

"It's bound," Matthew said.

Both men stared at him. His father's mouth opened, then closed.

Malcolm, of course, had a more practiced comportment. "The runes?"

"No. Ink," Matthew said.

His father frowned. "Like automatic writing?"

"No." Matthew showed his arm. "Tattoo ink."

"What?" The word seemed pulled from Malcolm Stirling. His carefully crafted mask of control slipped. Confusion and—more telling—anger flashed across his features. "What do you mean, *tattoo ink*?"

Matthew crossed the room to them, and held out his hand to his father. It took his father a moment to react, but he took his son's hand and shook. Matthew let the magic out, asking for the future of the one he was touching.

The triangle of ink on his forearm bloomed. The ink twisted and shifted in three directions.

"See?" Matthew said. "I'm in charge." He smiled as the two men stared, obviously unsure what they were seeing.

"Is that a puppet?" his father asked. On Matthew's arm a puppet was dancing, strings attached to one side of the triangle. From the second a snake twisted and tied itself in knots. From the final side, a frost pattern grew all the way to Matthew's elbow.

It made sense to him. His father hadn't been his own man in decades. He was trapped. He would never achieve anything, instead doomed to be as he was, a hollow man who—despite having magic—had no direction of his own.

"I think so," Matthew said. "Obviously, it'll take me time to interpret, but the dreams will stop. I won't go crazy." He let go of his father's hand. The ink collapsed back into the single triangle.

"How will you divine futures?" Malcolm Stirling asked. His voice was razor thin.

"I'm not sure I will," Matthew said. "But I can use it to learn a lot about the people around me. Figure out who to trust, who has the best interests of others at heart." He locked eyes with Malcolm.

The silence that followed his words lasted seconds.

Matthew exhaled. "If you don't mind, I'll go now. Binding the magic was pretty exhausting."

His father still looked shell-shocked, but his great-grandfather nodded stiffly. No doubt already trying to figure out a way to use this version of the gift to his advantage. Matthew didn't care. Malcolm could ponder all he wanted, the symbology the ink used wasn't a deck of Tarot or a bag of runes. It was his own.

Matthew left them and went to his bedroom. He stopped at the mirror beside his dresser and raised his hand to his shoulder, regarding his reflection. He put his hand where Jace's had settled earlier, and let the magic out, touching no one but himself.

A dragon slipped from the triangle, tearing through puppets and chess pieces and solid walls of brick, leaving only spinning clouds of dust in its wake. It snaked toward his wrist, wrapping around his arm and settled there, its long powerful body trailing up his arm. And beside it, all the way, ran a wolf.

Matthew looked at his reflection, and nodded.

Things were going to change.

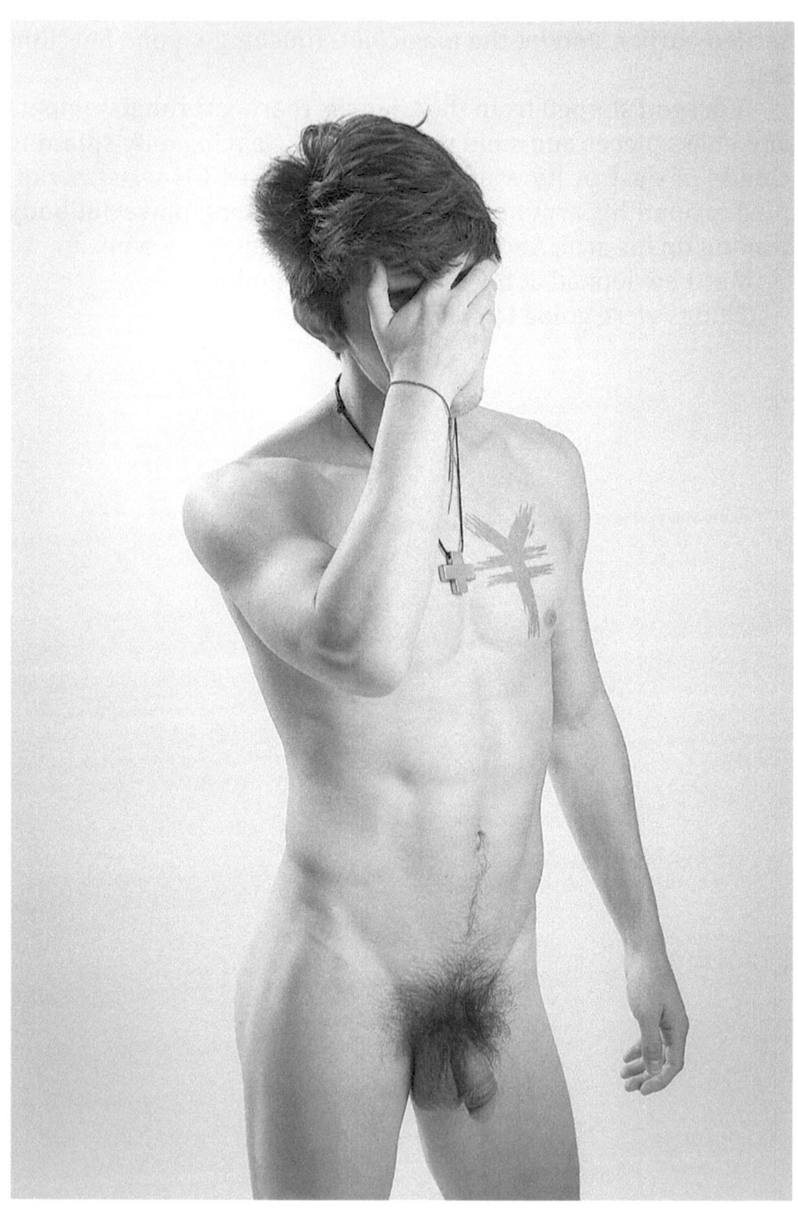

Yggdrasil

Mark Ward

His heart covered, his tattoo is shorthand;
unable to speak the language he points,
his chest doing all of the work. He can't

bear the salaryman working his joints.
Eyelids blink behind his hand, child-like
he lets the world mark his skin, anointed,

annotated, he stares at all the shrikes
through his fingers, emerging from his roots.
He is the gallows deciding to strike

back. The birds circle his body, their route
pushing the petrified client down past
the tree growing out from him now like fruit.

His branches break through the ceiling, the glass.
He removes his hands from his eyes, at last.

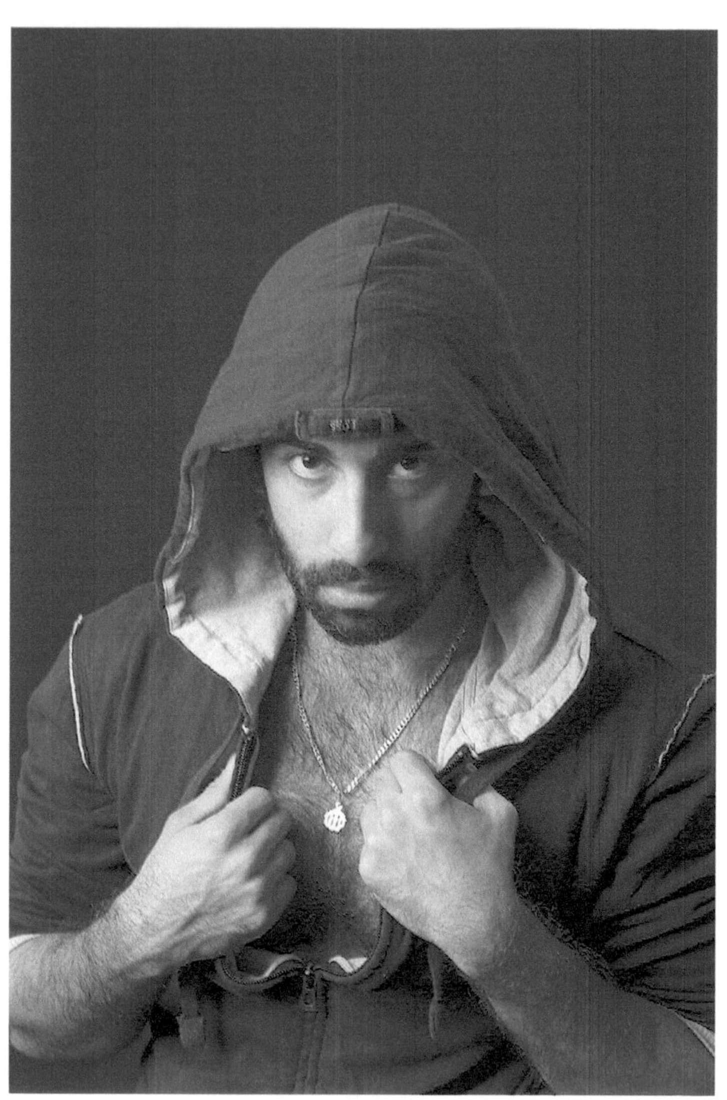

He-Witched

Gregory L. Norris

One of my biggest rules in life and romance is to avoid using love potions, no matter how tempted I am. Oh, they exist, but when it comes to matters of the heart, what's the point of love if it isn't genuine? When a tall, handsome stranger struts out of the woods while you're picking a bumper crop of vegetables and herbs from your garden, and you experience that rush of attraction and know he's feeling the same, how sweeter the deal when it's real.

I met Ben Stoddard on one of those perfect, transitional late summer mornings. Change was in the air. Sunshine spilled down in a muted, warm shower somewhere between the fiery orange of late August and the stark gold of the fall to come. Promises Kept, my cottage on five acres, was nestled against the big conservation woods. I had gathered ten giant tomatoes and some purple Perilla basil and was picking a bouquet of zinnias for the kitchen table when I sensed another's eyes on me. Turning, I tracked the glances to the wood line, where a figure stood at the head of the trail.

"*The Elk King*," I whispered.

It turned out not being the fabled guardian of the trees. Still, the man was a vision to behold—a buck with big antlers, I judged from a glace at the meaty fullness of his jogging shorts.

"Howdy," he said on the march over, waving a big, manly hand.

He had a boyish, handsome face; the rest was all-man: dark hair, close cut; eyes beyond blue to a deep shade of sapphire; long, lean torso clad in a dark gray hoodie and those jogging shorts; sneakers on big feet—a divine distraction.

"Well, hello to you," I said, trying to contain my smile.

My visitor lifted the bottom of his hoodie to wipe sweat from his face, which showed a prickle of five o'clock shadow at just after nine in the morning. I stole a look at the magnificent muscles of his abdomen. A trail of dark hair cut him neatly down the middle, stopping only to form a circle around his navel before plunging past the waistband of his underwear—boxer-briefs, black, I surmised.

He extended his hand. My heart galloped as I caught his scent on my next sip of air—clean male sweat, piney and fresh, magical. I attempted to swallow and nearly choked on the dryness in my mouth. Our hands met, mine vanishing in his. With little effort, I imagined him capable of shattering bones.

"Ben," he said, his voice deep and arousing. "Ben Stoddard."

I feigned coolness, ignored the flames consuming me inside. "Jesse Fox," I answered.

Ben's eyes fixed me with a look. I realized I was being studied with the same curiosity and—dare I think it?—the same *desire*.

"I saw you," he said and paused, as though carefully choosing his words. "From the woods."

"My very own stalker," I said lightly.

He laughed. We were still shaking hands. He broke the connection, and I regretted my little joke.

"No, nothing like that," he said.

"Really? A pity."

Our eyes kept the circuit. In that bottled gaze, electricity flowed.

"Saw you when I was jogging," Ben said. "I'm exploring all the trails up there."

He tipped his chin, indicating the woods. From somewhere in the lush green veldt, a mourning dove cooed its haunting sad song.

"I love those woods," I said. And then, not entirely sure why, I added, "Be careful of places where the trees grow so close together they block out the sun completely."

"Why?" he asked, a goofy smile on his boyish face. "Is the place haunted?"

"Something like that," I said. I should have elaborated, but all I could think of at that moment was how to get his smile on a daily basis.

"Well, young Mister Fox," Ben said.

"Jesse, please," I chuckled. "'Mister Fox' sounds so official."

"Good, Jesse, we're gonna be seeing a lot of each other."

"Really?"

"Yup."

He'd bought the old Bergeron house, the nearest of Promises Kept's few neighbors, and was planning to fix the place up.

"Are you a handyman?"

"I know how to use my power tools," he said and flashed a cocky grin.

Like I said, who needs love potions when old-fashioned hormones work wonders?

Ben pointed at the grapevine basket with the morning's harvest. "How about dinner sometime?" he asked.

"Dinner?" I parroted.

"Yeah. You and me. Tonight. Your place—mine's not ready for company yet."

"You should know I don't eat meat," I blurted out.

A smirk broke on Ben's mouth. "No? Sure I can't change your mind?"

The morning's temperature doubled. Words flew past my lips before I could trap them. "Tempt me."

He grinned, more a wolfish snarl than an actual smile. "Maybe I will. See you at five, Jesse."

He moved closer. I half expected him to kiss me and was disappointed when he didn't. Instead, he plucked a zinnia from the basket and slid it behind my right ear. His nearness mixed the fragrance of basil with his masculine scent. I worried that I might climax right there in the side yard, without need of further stimulation.

Ben turned and jogged away. I ogled the perfection of his athlete's legs, the full, almost square muscles of his ass, the damp line between the shoulders of his hoodie.

"I'm not sleeping with you on our first date," I called.

Ben turned and jogged in place. "Technically, dinner will be our second," he said, and offering nothing more than a cocky smirk, he ran back into the woods.

I stood rooted to the spot, speechless, my erection so thick it verged on painful. There were other dangers in the woods I should have warned him about, but Ben Stoddard was, I sensed, a man in control of his own destiny. *A man used to getting what he wants*, I thought as I crossed the threshold of Promises Kept.

*

I've used spells in the past. Number spells helped me earn enough money to buy my little cottage. Protection spells keep darkness from my door, working flawlessly my five seasons at Promises Kept.

I named the house after my own sacrosanct rules, the ones I refuse to break. I'd promised to harm none, and thus far had done a fine job of scooting spiders and moths out of the house. Not one of the bees in my apiary has stung when I harvested honey. I smudge the hive with sage, scattered with a turkey feather I found by the stream that tumbles past my garden. I never take more honey than I need.

"Ben, Ben, Ben . . ." I sang, as though his name were part of an incantation. I relived the encounter, cursed the slowness of the clock, and reminded myself how smart I was to avoid love potions and all the drama they create for the spell-cast and the spell-caster.

Change was in the air, both in the weather and in my heart. I baked herb bread, tidied the house, and caught lazy leers from Cheetah, my familiar, whose tail twitched as the old cat lounged on the bed.

"What?" I asked.

Cheetah yawned, her only answer.

*

A knock sounded on the front door. My heart jumped into my throat. Mustering the last ounce of coolness I had left, I answered. Ben stood there, that mischievous grin on his face. He'd shaved, but the shadow of his morning stubble persisted. Baby-blue button-down shirt, old jeans, new sneakers, baseball cap, the bill aimed backwards. He carried a ragged bouquet of coneflowers and wild asters.

"For you," he said, extending the offering.

"They're beautiful," I said, accepting.

He wandered into the cottage, growled something about the flowers growing in the overgrown gardens at the old Bergeron house, which he'd closed on a week before.

"What really convinced me was this place," he said, glancing around and taking stock of the comfortable furniture and knotty pine walls covered in framed botanical artwork. "You made me want to be your neighbor."

I put the flowers in my favorite vase, an antique coral ceramic in the shape of a harp that belonged to my great-grandmother Van Horn. I acquired much of my appreciation for the natural world from her.

"Something smells great," Ben said.

I wondered if he meant the herb bread, the summer berry parfait, or me. I began slicing one of the plump tomatoes on a plate. "It's going to be nice having you next door."

"Why's that?" He chewed a slice of the bread and licked his lips.

"You know, having a handyman, one who knows how to use his tools . . ."

We never made it to the salad, let alone dessert. Ben seized hold of me, cupped the side of my face with his hand, and crushed our mouths together. Clothes dropped along with inhibitions. By the time we reached my bedroom, where Cheetah watched from the reading chair unimpressed, Ben was down to that baseball cap and one fluffy white athletic sock, which tangled around his toes, refusing to come off. We fell on the quilt, touching, tasting. His tongue tested my mouth's willingness. I accepted. Tongues wrangled, hands explored. His hardness entered my softness, and we formed a male Yin Yang, a sacred geometry that lasted well into the night. Thunder crashed. A restless wind savaged the dark woods overlooking Promises Kept, and in my bed, a smaller but no less grand reenactment of the explosion that first gave life to the universe took place—four times.

*

"I like that you named your house," he said, shattering the silence that hung over the room.

"Houses have personalities, too," I said, caressing the medallion of dark hair on his chest. "They take on the energy of those who live within their walls."

I sensed Ben studying me. A little chuckle powered up his throat.

"What?" I asked, tickling him in a more sensitive spot.

He flinched, laughing. "Quit that."

"No. Tell me."

"Okay," he said and repositioned my fingers. "It's just that . . . *fuck* . . . all right, here it is: I don't think I've ever been happier."

I glanced up. In the light of the beeswax candle burning on the bedside table, I saw genuineness in his sapphire eyes. "Say again?"

"You make me very happy, Jesse Fox," Ben said.

Raindrops pelted the world beyond the bedroom window. The breeze returned, transforming the gauzy summer curtains into dancing Halloween ghosts. I scooted higher and pressed my lips to his, saying nothing. The universe exploded and was recreated a fifth time.

*

Happy, or happier than he could recall? I drifted in a place not quite awake or asleep. The statement worked both ways. Love at first sight, without spells, potions, or malice—I hadn't fully believed such a thing possible. Now . . .

I reached for the other side of the bed. My fingers brushed cold sheet. I opened my eyes to see that half of the bed was empty.

I sat up. Cool air spilled in through the windows. Ben stood between the billowing curtain-ghosts, his magnificent body naked, little more than a silhouette, a man half there.

"What you said to me today," he said. "About the woods."

I started to answer, only to suffer an unexpected chill that ran down my spine and spiraled deeper, beneath my flesh, in concentric ripples.

"You said something about the dark part of the woods. Avoiding places where the trees grow close enough together to block out the sun."

"It's a wise choice, yes."

Ben turned to face me. His eyes seemed to sparkle with a preternatural blue glow. "I saw something after you and I talked. Up there."

"What did it look like?" He hesitated. "Ben?"

He folded his arms. The curtains rippled in the restless wind. "A toad. A giant toad, big as a dog. It had a human face and was staring at me."

Another shiver threatened. I fought it. "Come back to bed," I invited.

Ben moseyed over. He pulled the covers up to his neck. He shivered, too, enough to make his teeth chatter.

*

I woke in the morning shadows before dawn, convinced the seasons had completed their transition. The world had changed. When I looked over, expecting to see proof of love at first sight, Ben was gone.

After a night filled with pledges of love and shows of passion, I woke to a house not only devoid of Ben but also missing any shows of affection. No note scrawled with hugs and kisses, no cell phone number scribbled on a scrap of paper. Even the flowers in Great-Grammy Van Horn's vase had started drooping. Cheetah sensed the wrongness in the air, and slinked around with her head held low and eyes wide, yowling.

The gray morning pressed against the house. I lit candles, chanted and prayed as I normally do, and attempted to bask in the afterglow of my night with Ben. He was a lover skilled beyond my expectations, striking a perfect balance between gentle and rough. While washing dishes, I relived one of our conversations.

"Favorite movie?" he'd asked.

"*Xanadu*," I said without hesitation. He shrugged. "With Gene Kelly and Olivia Newton-John as a muse who grants two men their fondest dreams."

"Never saw it."

I lifted to my elbows and studied him. "I didn't think you had."

"Why?"

"Because I'm a cat person, and you look strictly dogs—big ones. Let me guess—your favorite's a sports movie, right?"

"*Field of Dreams*, so?"

So, I thought, *opposites attract*, and there was plenty of hope for Ben and me. Except . . .

I remembered what he'd said about horrors in the woods, and wondered if there was a connection between that strange confession and his disappearance.

*

I bathed, using soap I made from lavender and wildflowers, and dressed. I selected one of my woven baskets and set out to my garden, where I gathered red peppers, fat tomatoes, sprigs of basil, and handfuls of snap beans. I cut the last of the blossoms from my tea roses, grabbed a jar of honey from the pantry, and headed up the trail into the woods.

The forest was eerily silent. No mourning doves cooed, and even the blue jays weren't squawking. The world seemed to hold its breath. Anticipation crawled over my flesh, and I was glad that I'd pulled on an old wool sweater to stay warm.

The trail, one of several weaving through the ancient pines and skeletal paper-white birches, forked. Right led deeper into the secretive veldt, and left snaked along the backyard of the old Bergeron house. The New Englander's flower boxes had sat empty for years. Now Ben had arrived and something new and beautiful blossomed as a result. I heard nails being hammered. New life beat within the house.

"*Ben*." I whispered his name, imagining carnal scenarios in which we blessed every room in his house after the same fashion we had my bedroom. Promises Kept was a small house, whereas the old Bergeron place had at least a dozen rooms, judging by its size.

I chuckled to myself and closed the distance through overgrown timothy and crabgrass, past the woodpile, and to the back door. My heart pounded to the swings of Ben's hammer.

I knocked, timing my knuckles around nail strikes. He didn't answer. I tried again. The hammering stopped, killed by a grunted, "*Fuck*!"

Footsteps pounded closer. Movement stirred behind the threadbare curtain over a trio of glass panes. The door opened, and the wrongness I'd felt all morning was given body in the shape of the man before me.

Ben was dressed in jeans and a dirty tank top. His sweat washed over me, but it no longer smelled fresh and magical. Shadows had leapt from the forest's depths and under his eyes. His whole appearance was disheveled, exhausted. *Dead*, declared my inner voice. The boyishness was completely gone from his face.

"Ben, hey," I said, trying to sound cheerful.

Ben's eyes narrowed into dark slits. "What do you want?"

"I . . ." I stammered. "Um, you left so early. And I wanted to give you this."

I raised the basket filled with the bounty of my land. Ben's eyes scanned the honey, the vegetables, and tea roses as though they were abominations.

He swung the hammer. The jar of honey exploded and the basket flew, spraying its contents across the ground.

"Ben," I gasped.

"Get out," he spat.

I glanced up and froze at the hatred in his expression. If looks could kill.

"You disgust me," he continued, and raised the hammer. Hesitation flickered in his eyes, and fresh sweat beaded across his forehead. My first sense was that he didn't mean it. My next was that if I didn't move—and quickly—my head would suffer the same fate as the jar of honey.

"Ben, what's wrong?" I attempted.

He surged forward, driving me several steps backward. All I saw was his hatred.

"Get out of here and don't come back," he growled. "If you do, *I'll kill you*."

I hurried away. He watched me, the hammer gripped like a weapon. At the tree line, I tipped a look over my shoulder right as he turned back to the house. A wisp of dark smoke hung about him, so faint I wondered if I imagined it. So I opened my third eye, which looks out from the soul, and there it was, wound tightly around Ben's throat: a collar of black energy. The wisp of smoke was a tether, a leash.

A chill rippled my flesh.

Someone had placed a curse upon my prince.

*

I returned through the forest, aware of the ominous in ways my love for Ben had blinded me to: the silence, the shadows, the slithering crawl of unwanted eyes upon me.

At Promises Kept, I was safe. Protection spells in the form of salt crystals buried at intervals and certain plants with mystical properties growing in sacred geometries kept the badness out. However, in the forest their protection was minimal at best.

I dug in my heels. A stink of swamp coiled around me, carried on the fingers of a slight, gray mist.

"Who are you?" I demanded.

The silence thickened, and then I heard a giggle, gloating and full of itself. I tracked the voice into the thickets, to an impossible image hiding behind a hedge of ferns. My stomach knotted at the repugnant sight: a toad, its sandstone-colored hide covered in bumps. The toad's face, as Ben had reported, seemed more human than amphibious, especially in the eyes. The toad's mouth opened. Its sticky pink tongue smacked at its lips.

The toad croaked.

Foolishly, I'd traveled light to the old Bergeron house. I reached for my throat. My fingers found the loop of cord where a malachite crystal hung. I hoped it would be enough.

The toad's tongue lashed out at me. I sensed its touch would unleash deadly toxins, but it struck an invisible barrier in mid-air, mere inches from my face.

"Clever," the gloating voice taunted.

"No, practical, as all magic should be. A means to an end in which *none are harmed!*"

The tongue drew back. "Oh, not that tired old chestnut again. To make an omelet, you have to break eggs."

"Ben isn't an egg," I fired back. "Release him from your curse, or I'll—"

"You'll what?"

"I'll stop you."

The voice laughed. "You? Pitiful excuse for a warlock, you don't deserve his love. It was my duty to take him from you."

The toad turned and hopped away, its inelegant mass kicking up leaves and needles and stirring the pungent odor of the forest floor. Among it was something chemical—like a man's cheap body spray. Gripping the malachite, I pursued.

"You aren't leaving," I said.

The voice laughed, its gloat rippling up into the trees. A thunderous cracking sounded overhead. I had time enough to look up before a canopy of thick boughs tumbled down upon me, pinning me beneath their mass.

*

My first thought upon return to consciousness was for the trees, those beautiful elders harmed by the dark warlock's magic. As I exited the shadows, tasting blood on my tongue, my heart broadcast a healing chant for the sap-blood flowing from cracked limbs, for their pain to evaporate. My own body had sustained cuts and bruises. My right ankle throbbed, but it appeared only sprained and not broken.

I limped home to Promises Kept, past the line of protection, and instantly felt better. My relief was-short-lived, for I sensed the wrongness following me. Check that. The wrongness was already there. Certain plants spaced out like a living force field had been ripped out by their roots and lay dying in clumps. Salt crystals had been exhumed and flung in wide orbits. A gouge from truck wheels cut across the side yard and through the garden.

"Oh, no," I gasped, and hobbled to the front door, which stood ajar.

My home had been turned upside down. While I was unconscious under the branches, mean hands had tossed furniture and smashed botanical prints. My great-grandmother's vase was in pieces. I imagined a big hand, swinging a hammer. Written in what appeared to be blood across a length of knotty pine were the words: "With love, faggot."

Glass frames can be replaced. Even the destroyed heirloom could be fixed. But my panic rose over thoughts of Cheetah.

"Girl?" I sobbed into the house.

I found her safe, cowering behind the upended sofa, and thanked the universe for its kindness. The red on the walls had been last night's summer berry parfait.

*

As the sun set on that ugly gray day, I moved around the property repairing defenses. Some fixes were easy—I kept salt crystals in a jar beneath the sink—others, like the decimated elfweed and moonflower plants, required greater care.

By dusk, I turned my attention to the house itself and did my best to put Promises Kept in order. Weary, I collapsed into bed. Cheetah joined me, and we huddled together, both of us sleeping with one eye open.

*

Some warlocks can be territorial, laying false claim to land and lovers that don't belong to them. Others, like the Toad, will go to any length, break any law, to steal what they want.

It took all of my resolve to not blame Ben. He had only recently arrived to the realm, and we had loved one another. That love was sincere; the ugly meanness wasn't. The Toad had leashed him with powerful dark magic, and I didn't know if I could free him. I woke beside loyal Cheetah, who I sensed longed for the lazy days of summer before our world was put in jeopardy. And I knew I had to try. None of this was his fault. But if the Toad chose to tug on that leash too hard . . .

"Ben," I said.

And, standing, I vowed to save him.

*

I slipped a tiny mirror into my pocket, along with a few other choice precautions. Confident the strongest protection spells had been reestablished around Promises Kept, and with my ankle healed through herbs and magic, I jumped onto my bicycle and peddled toward town. The tiny mirror made me mostly invisible, so I used the bike path to avoid being hit by a clueless motorist. I soon arrived downtown and reached into my bike basket for the daisy wrapped in silk.

I parked behind a bench in the town green and wandered through the village's business center. I passed by the bank, holding the daisy in my hand. I figured if a dark warlock had newly set up shop in town, he had to be a banker or lawyer. The petals retained their pristine color and vibrancy. Then I passed the offices of both local attorneys, but the daisy's virgin brightness endured.

I almost gave up. Then I spied a stark white building with tall glass windows. The shingle outside read: "Dudley Tilden Mortgage." I remembered Ben saying he had closed on the Bergeron house the week before, and knew I'd found the warlock's lair. The daisy confirmed my suspicion. As I approached the building, the petals curled up. At the door, the flower dissolved into dust.

Oh yes, I'd cornered him.

The offices of Dudley Tilden Mortgage thrummed with an undercurrent of malice. Air gusted around me as I opened the door and sucked a swirl of dead leaves into the building. Several of the precautions I'd brought along warned me of danger. A packet of powders vibrated in my back pocket. Salt crystals warmed almost to the point of searing. The greatest warning came from my heart.

The leaves stilled in the dead air beyond the threshold. The décor was minimalist, cold white floors and walls lined with black ginger jars on shelves. It was the sort of place where a dark warlock could make dirty deals to get rich, gain power, and satisfy petty carnal desires. I wondered how many families had suffered because of Dudley Tilden. I briefly opened my inner eye, aware of the danger, and caught glimpses of his hand in the sub-prime mortgage crisis. The filthy prick had gotten away without paying for his crimes.

The chemical stink I remembered from the woods burned in my next sip of air. The inner door opened and a man wandered out. He was short with a blotchy complexion and badly dyed sandstone-colored hair. His large butt was shoehorned into pinstripes, and he wore a tie with a fat knot. Had he not been so dangerous, I would have pitied him, maybe even been amused by his ridiculous, toad-like appearance. Only we were long past anything funny.

"I know you're there," Dudley Tilden said.

Sounds filtered through the jars, as though something evil stirred within each obsidian vessel. Tilden narrowed his gaze and zeroed in upon me.

"Oh, the power of invisibility. I haven't seen something so ballsy in years."

The black jars shrilled with inhuman voices. The tiny mirror in my pocket cracked. The voices stilled.

"There," my nemesis said and licked his toadish mouth. "Much better."

"We haven't been formally introduced," I said, reluctantly extending my hand. "I'm Jesse Fox. Welcome to our fair town."

Tilden eyed my offer warily. "I know who you are. *What* you are. I saw the way he looked at you from the edge of the woods," he huffed, dismissing me with a sour expression. "Like he could ever love anyone as ugly as you."

I looked at my hand, the offer ignored. So much for the easy victory I'd hoped. I shook out my fingers. "You're a terrible person, and you've done rotten things—here and elsewhere."

"Piss off."

"And you're going to fix it all—or else."

Tilden the Toad laughed, a high-pitched, unattractive sound that would have been better suited to a howler monkey than a toxic little amphibian.

"You think this is funny?"

Tilden spat. "The nerve! You come here to my sanctum—"

I could have reminded him he did the same to me. Worse.

"—but, yes, quite funny. Do come in."

He waved me toward the inner office. Just as Promises Kept had absorbed my personality, the Toad's seat of power crawled with his. The walls appeared white to the physical eye, but to the inner, third lens they were green and bumpy and undulated with malice. The furniture was modern and uncomfortable, the desk made of thick glass and chrome. Tilden waved me toward a seat and took his chair.

I sprinkled salt and rose petals across the seat. The cushion squealed, renounced its malicious pseudo-intelligence, and gave up the urge to trap me in its clutches.

"Clever," said Tilden, "but if you do any more cheap trickery in my domain, I'll reduce you to ashes."

I reclined in a jaunty pose. "Do your best."

"Do you doubt my ability?"

I examined my nails and addressed Tilden from the cut of my eye. "Yes. You see, I thought about our little encounter in the woods. It was very hit and run. You couldn't get away from me quickly enough."

"Maybe it's because you disgust me."

I thought of Ben, handsome Ben, who'd said the same thing. Lines of dialogue, rehearsed. "I think it's really because you're jealous."

"*Jealous*?" Tilden spat. "Of you?"

I tipped a look at his toady eyes. "You come here, meet that wonderful prince—so tall and sexy and complete—only he's not interested in you. Instead, he's attracted to a witch who refuses to harm any. Even you, a mean little toad."

Tilden slapped his hand on the glass desktop. A wet, sticky sound of suction cups echoed through the room. Thunder boomed beyond the windows.

"How dare you!" he roared. "And stop trying to bewitch me with your feeble glances! I warned you if you tried to sway me, I'd destroy you!"

More thunder crashed, and I realized the cannonade came from within the building's infected walls. Footsteps followed. A dark shape loomed behind me. Breaking focus, I turned to see Ben plod zombie-like toward us from the outer room. Dark circles ringed his eyes, an ashy gray pallor stained his flesh. Drool seeped down his chin. His hands extended toward me.

"Kill him!" the Toad commanded.

Ben's expression tightened. He shook his head the slightest, but was powerless against the puppet master pulling his strings.

"Or better yet, I should kill *him*, and leave you to mourn his loss for the rest of your miserable existence!"

Tilden the Toad tossed back his head and let loose with more of his hideous guffaw. I sensed that there would be an instant—a fractured second—when his guard would drop. As the dark leash tightened around Ben's neck, I reached into my pocket and scooped up the strongest magic I knew: every happy dream and inspiration I'd ever enjoyed, each happy purr and mewl from Cheetah, each sunny day, every joyous memory I'd ever experienced. Rounding out the body of white magic was the taste of butter cream frosting on birthday cakes, the life-giving orgasmic sparks delivered by Ben Stoddard, and the complete soundtrack to the movie *Xanadu*. The invisible, eight-pointed star of goodness I had conjured burned with a blinding effulgence. I prayed it would be enough and pitched it right into the Toad's cackling mouth.

Tilden tensed, swallowed.

Ben dropped to the floor, grasping at his neck as the leash tightened, strangled.

Like I said, I have promised to harm none, and until that moment, I had never cast a love spell. I wasn't sure it would work.

Tilden gagged on the star of goodness, attempted to vomit it up, only it was inside him now, and quickly began to unravel all the darkness flowing through the man's blood and soul.

"Ben?" Tilden gasped. Then he shaped his fingers like scissors and snipped the air.

The leash of smoke puffed and floated away, and Ben ceased struggling. I jumped from the chair and raced to his side. The hatred evaporated from his eyes, and they glowed again like gemstones.

"Jesse?" he said, the color returning to his cheeks.

He wrapped his arms around me and we kissed. "I'm here, babe," I said. "You're safe."

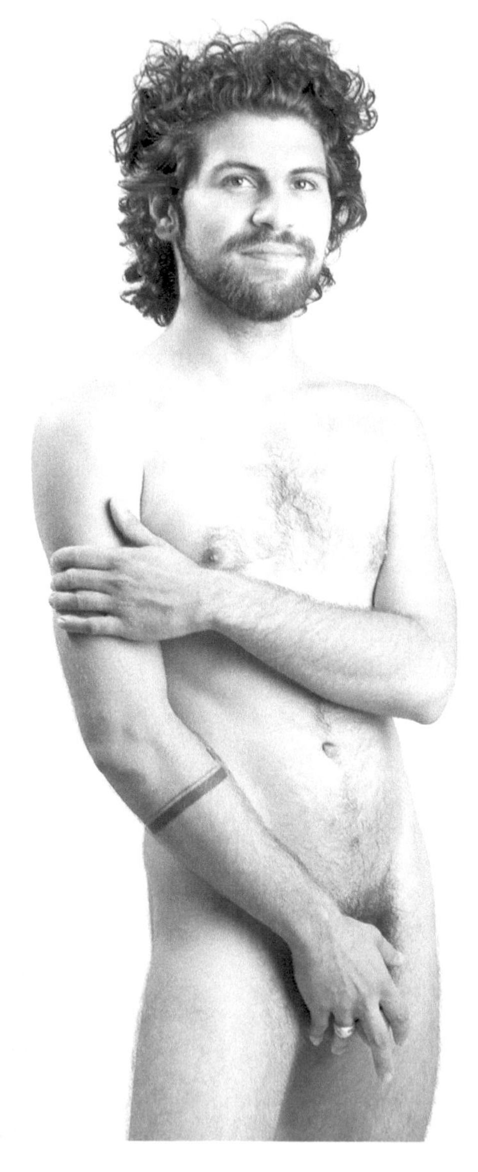

Django, Django, Thief of Hearts

Vinton Rafe McCabe

Django is seated behind the red pleated curtain. Only his shoes and the bottom of his brown trousers are visible in the place where that curtain does not touch the floor. His feet are careless, in one moment bent and pulled upward as if he were trying to reach en pointe, in another twisting in upon each other like a child's. His canvas shoes have seen better days. He wears no socks; dark hair twists upward from his anklebones into the cave of his pants.

The photo booth is tan, the aforementioned curtain the color of not-quite-dried blood; the whole of it is outlined in chrome, as if the thing had been cobbled together from an old Volkswagen van.

There is a flash, followed by a deep inhalation of breath from within the compartment, followed by a second low-wattage burst during which the booth seems to shift ever so slightly, and another in which his feet suddenly disappear, and another after which they return and play with the invisible pedals of an imagined car, and one last one that I believe is accompanied by a snicker.

There is then, I think, silence from within—hard to discern in the din of the arcade. His feet press hard against the floor of the booth.

I am growing impatient. My heart is pounding.

With a *whirrrr*, the small strip of black-and-white photos conveys itself from a slot, is cut by an invisible blade, drops into waiting hands.

"Are they okay?" asks a voice from within the booth.

I study them, eyes dipping down, rising up again.

"Oh, Django," I say *sotto voce*.

When he had at last told me his name just a few hours ago, he had leaned forward toward me until our noses nearly touched, and his eyes, his sweet, wide-open eyes filled the whole of the world for a thunderous moment and he whispered his name in a candy-sweet sigh.

Rearing suddenly, he continued: It's a gypsy name. Means full of life!

That word *life* glinted off his teeth as he bit down on it.

As he pulled back his eyes disappeared into the shadows of his brow.

"Let me see," he hisses from within, his right foot tapping silently with its rubber sole.

And a pale hand reaches out from the booth.

I lay the pictures on his outstretched palm.

After a moment: "I like the one where my dick is hard. Those ones are always the best."

I wanted to say, *not me, not me*—I like the one where you leaned in against the camera like you once leaned in to me. The one where your eyes make the camera want to weep. The one where your face, your face, the whole of it with the edges blurred and softened by extending beyond that shallow focus of the shot, gives access to your soul, permits me to stare.

But I say, "Yeah, you cannot beat a hard, hot dick." And let it go at that.

Django shoves the curtain aside quite suddenly and, rising up to his full height—a head taller than me at least—strides from the booth, the fingers of his right hand checking to see if his zipper is zipped as he hands me the photos with his left.

"Where to now?"

*

When I first laid eyes on him, he was twirling slowly underneath a cumulus of hair.

In his pink spotlight, he looked like the plastic ballerina in a girl's jewelry box, twirling endlessly to "Laura's Theme."

The glitter in his hair and on his chest rainbowed violet, blue, gold. His eyes looked upward into the light as he danced, quite ignoring the rhythm of "MacArthur Park." His hands twisted about in serpentine, like Norma Desmond inhabiting Salome, as he slowly, slowly twirled.

I looked up at him and rolled the cold sweat of the bottled Rolling Rock up against my hot forehead.

The nail of the thumb of his left hand, I noticed, was mashed inward, the nail bed deeply bruised. It looked as if he wore nail polish of a dark, vampish sort.

Surely it hurt; but his face was serene as he stared into the light.

As he was platformed, upraised, I stood at the level of his crotch, which was covered in a tiny pair of silver shorts that undulated as he turned, the front of them the green light that led Gatsby to the slaughter, as he rotated again and again. When I'd learned his name. When I'd synchronized my heart with his.

*

Offstage, at the deli devouring a chicken liver sandwich, or, before that, at the arcade, sitting in the photo booth just before he pulled closed the red curtain, he reminded me of when Marilyn Monroe was photographed reading Schopenhauer.

*

Once, out on the street, with throngs all around us, he spontaneously danced a bit more, to the music of some distant boombox that only he could hear. His hips registered the rhythm first, then his slim arms upraised themselves snake-ishly, then his toes curved downward to draw circles in the filth. He bit his lower lip; his eyes were suddenly as big as Betty Boop's on this hot August night.

*

Things I forgot to ask:

—Do you believe that Carter should have entrapped himself in the Rose Garden after the Iran hostage crisis began, making himself the 53rd hostage? Follow-up: Do you believe that that cost him the election?

—Dogs or cats?

—What is your position on the subject of abortion?

—What color handkerchief would you wear in your back pocket?

—How do you take your coffee?

—Have you ever loved, truly loved? If not, why not? If so, who, when, and how?

*

The best quote of the night: Trying to tiptoe into his personal life, I asked if he was, as such dancers often are, working his way through college.

He considered the question for a moment, before—looking down on the top of my balding head from his great height—saying, "I am working my way through *life*."

And he tossed an invisible scarf across his shoulders and around his neck like Isadora surely did when climbing into that Bugatti in order to drive home his point.

*

The happy, happy moment: me standing there holding the photo strip, full face, right profile, left profile, enormous dick jutting from a soft cloud of chestnut hair, slit smiling a Mona Lisa smile. Him asking, before I have to wheedle, before I have to beg, "Where to now?" As if he wanted my company, as if I'd somehow earned it.

Then us leaving the arcade. Us walking down the street to the deli two blocks down. Him, hungry; me, flummoxed. We walked: Mutt & Jeff, Chip & Dale, Amos & Andy, Damon & Pythias, David & Jonathan.

And I felt the feeling of skin on skin when quite suddenly he laid his hand tight, grasping, on top of my wrist and steered me slightly to look into a store window where leather sex masks were laid out on display. He tilted his head appraisingly, like the RCA Victor dog as he gazed within. He sighed and turned to me with a mouth grinning a field of white teeth and then winked one gigantic eye.

A happy, happy time.

*

The things I learned about him:

—That Django wears only two kinds of footwear: Huaraches in daytime; Converse All-Stars at night. He never wears socks.

—That he has been a vegetarian for two or three years now, but is seemingly unaware (at least when we were ordering down at the deli) that chickens are in the category of animal, not vegetable.

—That, even when he has been dancing for several hours, his energy is boundless. He smells like vanilla beans that had been roasted slowly in the oven, then combined with the scent of rare exotic Portuguese paprika, and both mixed with the damp odor of hemp.

—That he has seen *The Blue Angel* repeatedly, every time it is shown at an art cinema. And that he admires mightily the artistry of The Cockettes.

—That no one else, not on all of God's green earth, loves so much to laugh as Django does, or laughs more fully, more completely, with tiny joyous orgasms erupting all over his body. And that he amuses himself far more than I do.

—That Django may or may not be his real name.

*

Goldblatt's Deli, an ode, an elegy, and a pensée, all at once:

His fingers plunked like rhythmic raindrops on the plane of sticky Formica.

The menu was slight, only one photocopied page in a clear plastic sleeve, but he studied it as if it were the Rosetta Stone and he were rapt in translation.

It was dinner, after all.

*

Flashback to the Club:

The invitation to dine extended; the invitation to dine accepted. He looked as if he could use a good meal. He looked as if he were unlikely to say no.

He, twirling twirling looked down at the top of my head when I, during the interval between Cher and more Cher (the second, "Gypsies, Tramps and Thieves," seemed most apt), called up at him "May I take you to dinner?" in what I thought was the proper tone of supplication. He then seemed lost in thought for a turn or two before he raised a single eyebrow and gave me a nod of the greatest beneficence, the vaguest of yeses, but a yes nonetheless.

And I retired to the bar and to a series of Long Island Iced Teas while I watched him, becoming squeamish with delight each time he spun like a lighthouse so that the bright lights of his eyes pointed in my direction.

Once, a MAN approached him.

The dancer at once stopped his dance and bent down on bended knee, although he seemed less to be issuing an invitation than receiving one. The MAN, all bulky, inky, and scruffy in his unquestionably tight tight jeans, so taut over the area of the crotch and muscular thighs that the brute's undulating walk could have easily resulted in spontaneous combustion.

The MAN whispered in what I assumed was a low, glottal growl and pressed himself as best he could against the boy, who rested his wispy hands on the MAN's bulging arms, tracing the outline of the word "Mother" with his thin forefinger.

They disagreed. MAN, it seemed, said *yes yes yes*; boy, apparently, countered *no no no*. Admittedly, the boy's hand remained on the *Mother* arm throughout.

Django slowly shifted his weight and began to rise up again into his pink spotlight.

The MAN grabbed his wrist and held it.

Django covered the MAN's hand with his own, then shifted over and, slipping his hand under the MAN's own, lifted that heavy pork chop to his lips and kissed it. I breathed in and out to the length of the kiss. One breath. Two. Three. I feared hyperventilation.

Django patted the MAN's hand and returned it.

And slowly weaving back and forth, back and forth, his snake arms upraising, Django regained the spotlight. He shrugged at the MAN *what can you do?* and then pointed over across the floor to where I was sitting. It seemed he bobbled his head a bit. I raised my glass in salute. And the MAN walked into the darkness of the dance floor, which was crowded, sweaty-wet, and most congenial.

While waiting for Django's shift to end, I danced a bit myself with a man named Earnest, who attempted to tell me his life story at the bar. He sat down next to me, his stomach sort of deflating as he sat, and started in, his eyes moist as he spoke of young love and the Old South. After the bit in which he revealed that he had moved to the coast several years before because of his deep yearning for cock, I suggested that undulation would help his tale go down. And so we took to the floor.

In that Earnest had several years and many pounds on me, I did not think that Django would object to my bit of entertainment. And, indeed, he never seemed to notice.

All I saw of him on his pedestal was the glinting of his silver mini-shorts as he gyrated and bobbed.

*

When at last he was ready to leave:

I was back, seated, Earnestless, at the bar, and I must admit, quite inebriated. Did I leer? Did I drool?

Because he was suddenly *there*, stuffed into those brown pants, his white shirt still damp from where he had attempted to wash the glitter from his chest. His glorious hair ensnared in a light blue handkerchief.

"Where to now?" he asked. "I'm starving."

"Goldblatt's?"

"Oh, excellent! Oh, yes, that's just fine."

And he placed an arm loosely around my shoulder, perhaps concerned that, left to my own devices, I might soon collapse on the pavement as we went out into that summer night.

On a whim, he suddenly steered me into the busy, noisy, smelly arcade that we were passing and maneuvered me over to the photo booth in the back, all with the promise of a gift, which I paid for with some quarters that I somehow managed to slip *one two three four* into the slot on the side of the thing with giddy, drunken hands.

*

At the table in Goldblatt's:

He takes my right palm in his hand, turns it upward and bends it flat, and, with that same slim forefinger that outlined *Mother* on the MAN, tickles my fate:

"I learned how from my grandmother Mafalda," he says as his fingernail carved what he said was my love line.

"Oooo la la," he says with a wink and a whistle.

Inopportunely, the waiter arrives at that moment with ice water. He seems not, I suspect, to like his job.

"I want chopped chicken liver on rye with sliced onion." Django tells him. "And a bowl of mixed pickles. And some cole-slaw. And iced tea." He lifts his ice water and drinks it down. "Could I have more water?" he asks. "And a black and white cookie?"

He holds my hand throughout, sandwiching it between his own.

"Coffee, please," I tell the man.

"And some pie. He'll have some Boston cream pie."

To me he whispers, "It's good here."

The waiter writes and then clips his pen to his pad.

"And could we have a plate of French fries for the table?" Django asks the back of his head.

"Now where were we?" He turns his attention back to me. He lifts his hand and points again at my palm.

"Ooooo la la," he said again with a wink.

The waiter reappears with the iced tea, my coffee, and a bottle of catsup and disappears again.

I want to say, *Don't ever let go of my hand*.

Instead, I say, "Yes?"

His eyes, I decided, had inlaid glitter all their own. And how I wished at that moment for some trick of the light from the faux stained-glass lights hanging overhead right there in Goldblatt's Deli to bring such a transformation in mine as well.

"Yours is a hand of passion, my friend." He flippers my flat palm, twists it side to side, brings it up in front of his face to study it in *bas relief*. "The heart line, the line of romance, is long and deep as a river gully. It shows many loves, many encounters of the heart."

"These lines," the outer side of my palm is twisted upward at the outside, allowing me to view its rim, "reveal that you will have three children."

"Only through a true miracle of God."

"Hush!"

The fries arrive piled high on a platter and are placed in the center of the table.

He grabs a few and jams them into his mouth before continuing.

"But beware in matters of love. You are surrounded by those who will not return the passion you feel for them." His voice is muffled by partially masticated fried potato.

I find this utterly charming.

Asked if he is a for-real gypsy, he reveals his last name to be *Roma*.

"I will keep my hand on my wallet and my eye on my watch." I laugh.

"Better you protect your heart." He snickers, curling my hand and sliding it back to me across the table.

He drumrolls with his index fingers as the rest of his food arrives along with my pie.

We chit and chat while the waiter clears his plates—for such a skinny boy, is he so very, very hungry. I sip coffee and allow it to be refilled with the waiter's every return, which results in brief sparks of clarity that penetrate my alcoholic haze.

Despite my questions, somehow he does not tell me where he lives or why he dances. Or where he is from, although I hear a trace of the flat Midwest in his voice. Instead, his reminisces are of the Old Country and Mafalda, who, in his telling of her, reminds me of Maria Ouspenskaya, and his life of the plot of some old werewolf movie.

The waiter collects some plates. Things clatter loudly.

Django eyes my pie.

I slide it across to him.

Django lustfully consumes my pie.

The light from the faux Tiffany stained glass overhead seems to be getting brighter.

I have a moment in which all things, all the threads, hand-tinted and hand-spun, that were woven into the weave, the roads taken and not taken, decisions made and decisions ducked, money spent and money saved *all all all* come together in this time and place. And I see him *very clearly*, with the bite of pie he had recently scooped: then teetering on his diner fork, now visible in his mouth as he chews and hums quietly and somewhat tunelessly.

Everything predatory within me shouts *Do It!* Everything avaricious cries *Do It Do It Do It Now!*

I see myself as if from a great distance. I see the index finger of my right hand dip into the chocolate frosting on the pie. See it point at the boy's face, move across the table to that face, see it smear the chocolate roughly on his lips. See the startle in his eyes. Feel the heat of his breath on my hand as with the chocolate I brand him.

I hear myself rasp, "*Mine*," still pointing directly at him. I speak in a voice that is not my voice, words shaped by lips that are not my own. Not mine. Octaves lower. More important—more insistent, more demanding, more *full throttle*.

I grab his wrist.

He drops his fork.

The moment is here. It is here and it is now and it is the moment. I feel my face flush. My short-sleeved cotton shirt is wet with sweat.

I take him. Right there, on the Formica table in Goldblatt's Deli, the faux Tiffany light with the cheap stained-glass cover witnessing the violation.

I rip his clothes off with my teeth and I say to him *there there* and then I lay him naked on that table. I nose against the whorls and wisps of downy hair that grow sporadically on his concave chest. I press my chin against his protuberant ribs. A hard prong, insistent, red, rises up between his legs, pushing me away.

Using Boston cream as lubricant, I rejoice in the act of penetration. Feel the hot gypsy blood course throughout his body. Hear his ragged gypsy breath. Notice the shudder as I repeatedly thrust. Lick the salty skin of his cheek, his forehead, his eyelid. And then witness his wide gypsy eyes go glassy as we finish together.

He lies there after, panting, staring up at the bulb in the faux Tiffany lamp as I zip up my fly.

And then, bidding the waiter over and borrowing his pen, I write, *Sorry, I guess I just don't love you* over and over and over and over on the taut skin all over his body.

*

His plate empty, Django smacks his lips and drops his fork with a clank. He motions the waiter.

"Could I have some coffee now?" he asks. He bites his lip. "Better make it decaf."

He glances over to me. "Do you want some more?"

"Yes," I say, sitting bolt upright as I put my quivering hands out of sight in my lap.

*

When I stopped by the front counter to pay the bill:

After I had offered him some mints from the bowl by the register and he had refused, and when we had finally walked out of the deli, I awaited another insouciant *Where to now?* I fully expected it this time.

But instead, from that great height that he stood above me, his moist, pursed lips reached down to kiss the top of my head, as a Spaniard does his darling child, not once but many swift, chaste times, *smack smack smack smack smack smack smack. Smack.*

And then the lips flew aloft once more with one brief gentle caress of my pate from his soft soft hand.

"Hey, thanks," he said simply. "Enjoy the pictures." He put his hand over the row of photos that stuck out of the chest pocket of my short-sleeved plaid summer shirt, which is to say, he put his hand for a moment over my heart.

Then he pulled his blue bandana from his head and his cumulus hair was lifted in a sudden summer breeze, showing the glitter that remained, that the rag had hidden.

Rainbows again. Violet, indigo, hot pink. Rainbows scattered in the neon light as he shook his hair free of the cloth.

And he tucked his bandana in his right rear pocket, a broad corner showing, and, unbuttoning his shirt to show his chest to the night, sauntered off through the shimmer of neon signs in windows and above doors, coloring flecks of the world in emerald and orange, lemon and old rose, through which he drifted down the hot, sweaty summer street and off into the darkness beyond.

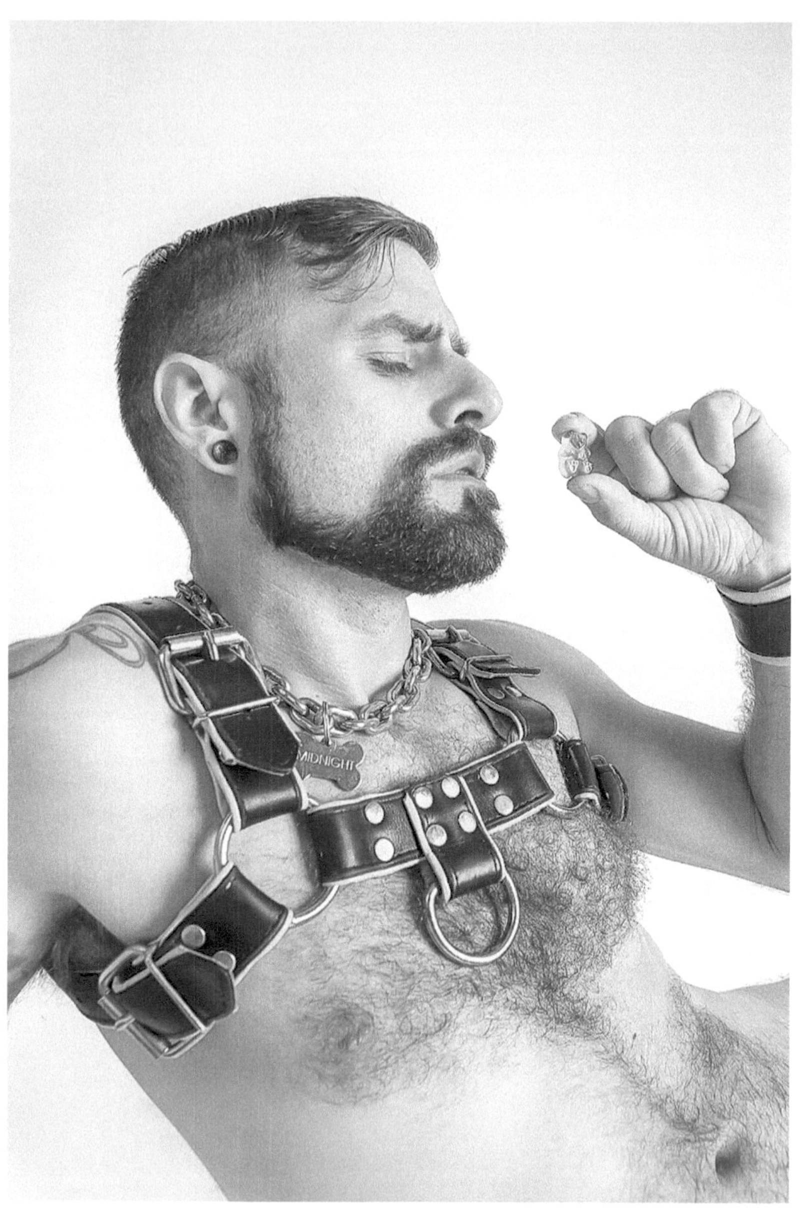
MIDNIGHT

Beastie Boys

Daniel Allen Cox

Boy light, boy bright, why did you refuse my whiskeyed
    spit tonight?
Still had to spackle it in.
There wasn't any lube
You said we could use Beastie Boys instead
And I said damn, I was planning to lose that iPod inside you.

Drop it up, drop it up, you kept saying
Like you couldn't understand gravity or men
Or ley lines.
Any ill communication when baking a fist in your gut
And it could go completely sideways.

Sip it in, sip it in
That's what I said when you were splayed and howling.
Be the seat buckle you were always meant to click with
What? To riddle you like you had riddled me
Ankle spurs through the cranium get me cranked.

Didn't believe a fist could disappear
So I opened my hand.
Your face took the shape of a star
Or maybe my fingers took the shape of your eyebrows
I cried and told you it was just arthritis & the news.

We were playing.
Wanted you to be shyer somehow, and louder

So we could pretend more things, and horsetail our mysteries.
Boy light, boy bright, close around my wrist tomorrow night
And I'll find my own way to your pulse.

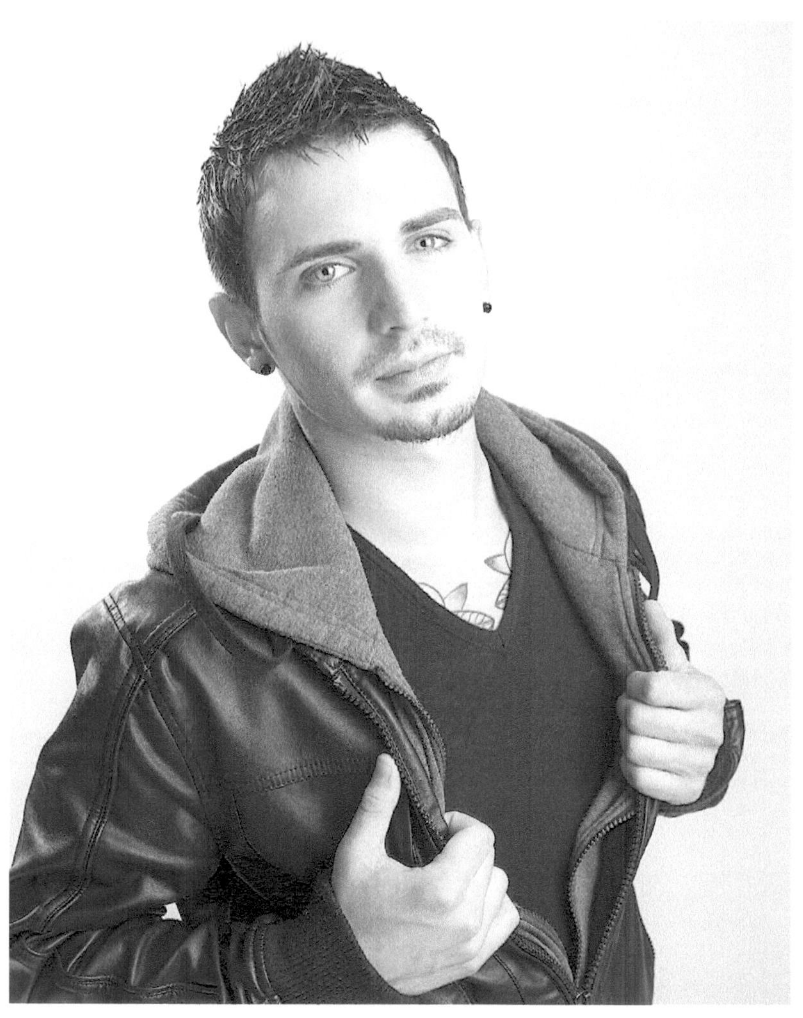

After Russian Hill

Michael Carroll

These aren't the true tropics but the subtropics, islands curving south from the boot-toe of the Florida peninsula in a meandering, westward-yearning ellipsis of archipelago--the last habitable coral chunk of which is Key West: bright sun by day, cloud-ragged moon at night.

Owen begins an afternoon by sunscreening himself and leaving his little home in the Old Town to wander toward Fantasy House, where for the first few hours he drinks nice iced tea. His refills are free and with every refill he tips two dollars. It's an all-male, clothing-optional, motel-like facility—compound really. Some guys never leave until it's time for the airport again. Why not, with the prettiest boys in town working here, serving and cleaning in their shorts and tees?

I can see him, all charm, establishing eye contact with each waiter: "Thank you, babe."

They take his two bucks, smiling, infected by his cheer, imparting some vague promise.

His Chuck has been gone for ten years. After San Francisco, Key West made sense. The investments accrue outrageous dividends, although this bubble—stretching to a point surely soon to break—frightens Owen. Chuck taught him that there would be good times and bad times, and that one's apocalyptic vision was part of the expected cycle. That capitalism's triumph depends on twitchy investors' fears. A nervous dare, a zero-sum game falling on his side for the moment.

When Chuck was in San Francisco Medical Center, he told Owen a lot of things, some of them pretty crazy and nearly Dada-surreal (the morphine). He also told Owen to weigh financial advisors' sage observations and experiences. Chuck was a whiz with money and Owen a former waiter who'd escaped the south hoping to become a photographer, too timid to try New York and thinking that San Francisco was just as good for what he wanted to do. Photography became his hobby, once he'd thrown me over after grad school for his First Republic Bank executive. Then becoming a rich, decorative housewife almost immediately became his vocation. I did worry. I would remind him from time to time he should have chucked it all (including, especially, Chuck) and moved with me to New York where both our careers would thrive (mine never did, while his default bloomed like cherry trees in the Japanese Tea Garden of Golden Gate Park). I'd stopped all the razzing and wheedling of Owen after Chuck was diagnosed. I could see it in his gunshot eyes, he'd truly loved Chuck, and I'd been a schmuck. I'd been more than a little self-righteous. I'd been manipulative, lacking in compassion, and following Chuck's painfully protracted death I went into a period of mourning parallel to Owen's. One that it took me a long time to disclose.

After all, Chuck had taken on Owen's Academy of Art debts and rarely cheated on Owen.

There is more than a little backstory due upon signing of this author-reader contract.

Some notes. Owen, despite no longer being auburn, remains resplendent. What the boys working at Fantasy House don't or can't see in Owen must have to do with their heterosexuality.

That is, some of them do gay-for-pay (common knowledge), but Owen would never pay.

I daydream. For instance, that I might not now be sick if before I'd scored Owen's love.

Or that he might never have lost Chuck somehow. I was always willing to share.

The trope of the enduring difficulty of saying you're sorry often featured in pop songs is, in fact, not cheap—but what the functional alcoholic Noël Coward was referring to in his famous bon mot: "Extraordinary how potent cheap music is." Actually Coward was quite a popster, too.

I myself am an alcoholic, recovered, but am not sure that the unrecovered Owen is or has ever been an alcoholic. However, as usual, I may be idealizing him.

But I do see him there. The pool is rectangularly ringed with chaises longues of a solid, ergonomically giving, blood-orange foam. From time to time he moves out from his table under the bar shelter to sit in the sun and drink more of his iced tea and check his messages and maybe even read. He brings a canvas tote from home carrying middlebrow "literary fiction" titles inside but none that I wrote—since those novels (and I mean all of them) have never been published.

He's watching the time on his phone when he can order the first drink, usually a glass of chardonnay, though this will often progress in the next hour to mixed drinks or straight liquor.

Chuck used to chide Owen for having a glass of white wine before six, which only made Owen frequent bars in the early afternoon while Chuck was at the office. I used to go with him. Owen was most jubilant when Chuck was out of town on business. Cheating for Owen was bars, not sex. Cheating for Owen meant getting away with afternoon drinking—that much he told me.

I see him but don't know what he's thinking, and never did. Is he wondering if he should take out his camera and immortalize these beauties, as he once did for his Academy of Art thesis, when he and I used to wander down to the strip clubs South of Market? The boys would rush up to him the minute we came through the door and fight with one another to be the next subject for their nerdy Jimmy Olson. He would offer each several twenties of Chuck's money, which they'd rarely take, just as Owen never took any of them up on their offers of sex in their Mission rooms.

He thought they should be paid for the privilege of having them pose for him. Of course, I'm no fortuneteller but I think they were holding out for a much bigger payday, as they are here.

On my last visit to Key West, I never once saw his beautiful Nikon bazooka, the one that Chuck had bought him on a trip to Tokyo. Everything for Owen was perfect because of Chuck.

When I asked him about the Nikon, Owen said, "I still have it but I never think about it."

I asked myself what he did think about, but Owen isn't the type to anticipate thoughts.

Chuck used to say, "Owen's a beagle, friendly to everybody, but he always comes home."

When Chuck died, Owen put their two beagles, Georgia and Stieglitz, up for adoption.

My father earned a merit badge in hunting-dog husbandry, and I know from his anecdotes that beagles are really famous for going off with any old stranger that reaches out to them.

Last note: as a former English major and creative writing MFA flop, I have a special spot in my heart for the typographical colon, be it via Forster or Capote. So you'll see some of those.

Owen's never been good for a whole lot, but he has fun with people. Likes meeting new ones, and running into the old ones. For fifty, he knows, he's holding up and people gravitate toward a youngish face and fast smile. At Fantasy House there is a steady source of guys. They fly down from all over, but too there are regulars who live closer to this archipelago, up in Tampa-St. Pete, Miami, Clearwater, the Panhandle and Jacksonville. Go back to Jacksonville and he'd hole up in an apartment in San Marco or Riverside, leafy neighborhoods the people living outside of which border on sketchy-hard. Folks there stay at a full, resentful boil—Christians and libertarians with anger issues, and deeply held convictions manifesting most innocently as yard nativities, and less innocently as all kinds of phobias. Think they can reprogram the peter. You don't get that here.

You get the neighborly stereotype of the south, mealy-mouthed but well-meaning, polite.

You walk in the front door and because you don't look like a gay Q-Tip and your face has not utterly collapsed and your neck isn't turkey-scrawny or slumped like Christmas pudding they wink, the older managing staff. They say, "Hey, Owen—'s going on, you keeping 'em honest?"

Not for a minute do they think he's any randy tiger. Maybe they respect him. Or maybe they're just waiting for him to have a spectacular shit-show night so they can start to ignore him.

"Need anything, babe?" he hears from the mature ones working the front desk or the bar.

The whole compound's frankly lewd and sometimes they'll ask, "See anything you like?"

Meaning the kids, reprobates and rent boys and Gothy hooker drag types. Or now, those completely well-adjusted gay spring breakers, very beautiful boys who never knew shame. Who rent the house next door to Owen and act like boys in their woodsy clubhouse: *Treasure Island*, tropical foliage, trees and bushes and vines and flowers growing out of every crevice. One day they climbed the gumbo-limbo to the roof to tan and ended up horsing around on the hot slippery tin, and Owen stopped on his porch to watch. He had been airing out the pillows and remembers clutching a slightly sour-smelling sofa cushion to his chest, mesmerized. That night he dreamed Chuck was teaching him to make a chicken tagine. In the dream, Chuck said, "You never liked coriander root, but it's essential to the recipe. Also, you refused to sleep with that Moroccan kid and me but I know you peeked in." Only the thing about the kid in Morocco had ever happened, not the cooking, and it had happened a while ago. When it happened, he'd talked to Denise.

Denise would say, "Why didn't you join them? You said the kid was attractive."

"It was wrong for me, but not for Chuck. Darling, you know I'm not made like that."

"What are you made like then?" she said. "I've been trying to figure that out forever."

She'd already moved to New York, and he phoned her at midnight eastern time to say he was thinking of leaving Chuck and had been thinking of leaving him ever since their flight from Marrakech and the connection in Paris bringing them back to California. He couldn't count the number of cigarettes she was lighting and smoking in the course of the conversation, though he was sure it had to be a lot. It always took a lot, with Owen. He had been careful not to suggest that he might move to New York and join her, sure that he'd stay in the Bay Area until he died.

He said he wouldn't tell Chuck what he was considering until he'd ultimately decided.

Maybe that's what haunted him about the dream with Chuck, his self-avowals. Like the needless one never to come on to any of these boys, though he had plenty of money to make that happen. He didn't grow up poor, but he didn't grow up with enough to make him, as his family called it, "comfortable" either. He doesn't deserve it. He's never deserved the recreational sex Chuck needed and could afford after losing interest in being physical with Owen. Owen had lost interest, too, but in everybody. Everybody because he was afraid one breach of their relationship (breach in his mind) would have him out on the street: give Chuck an excuse to eject him finally.

Denise used to get exasperated with him on this count. The go-go boys South of Market fawned all over him, and if they weren't devils (they were adorable but often fucked up, and they had their issues as runaways and rejects), they were sticky temptations with money issues. He'd never put himself above them, yet maybe this psychologizing of them was telling, too.

When he first visited Key West after Chuck's death, there was, briefly, a boy go-go bar on Truman named Scooter's. He never went in, and since his first visit (when he stayed in a cramped corner room of Fantasy House) Scooter's has closed, along with its sister establishment, a titty bar. He would sooner have entered the titty bar than Scooter's. Having grown up Pentecostal, he is residually superstitious. His go-go boy obsession may have given Chuck his abdominal cancer. From experience, he knows marital neglect can be toxic. Now the stuccoed cement-block building has become on one side a liquor mart and on the other a sex shop, a development that nonetheless comforts him.

In the decade since he's lived here, he's heard locals complain about changes, the changes that mark the town's transition from marginal hedonistic hot spot where anything goes to just one more corporately exploited, condo-covered resort. Owen's just invested in a condo development.

He has to come to terms. He has to face the future. Maybe one affair with a troubled kid from Chattanooga and he'd be happy. He could help turn that kid around.

He would never say "affair," not to me. With me he'd likely throw out the word *fling*.

After that whopper of a condo goes up, he might push on to Palm Beach, "get with it."

He jacks off at night and again in the morning, recovering from his white wine hangover. He looks up "skinny boy" and Googles "homeless gay" and has even been known to type "waif" and "scally." A scally's a British punk, bordering on an English neo-Nazi, who likes to be rough and curse you, spit on you, slap your face, choke you and whip your bare ass with the leather belt you hand him upon command. He makes you buy him a Burberry raincoat and scarf, before he's agreed to meet you, making you pay for your erotic greed. You don't deserve him and you better have that fucking Burberry ready before he can think of kicking the shit out of and fucking you.

No scally lads down here but what you get for rough trade is other runaways and confused little bastards who come on sweetly, not paying, though they may first enter by scrounging up the cash for a day pass just to get in, get into the brains of those who pay, and get into the interior culture.

They're here for the older ones, many on pensions and social security, the hopeful and the otherwise disabused, some with money for an all-inclusive package—queer lepers no matter how you slice it, since to be here and to count is to have gay coin, hard-earned or shadily gotten, or to be young and hot but in any case to have one of these assets or the other. These johns fly at half-mast freely, their hides deep-tanned and slack. Their dongs are numb major-size puds or cocktail weenies, their asses hang from them like the undefined seats of old underwear, and Owen knows he's got something like that on him in the future. Hats off to them, he thinks, for crossing a line he'll never cross. It's enough to watch and to learn from their living, and he doesn't judge them.

Everybody looks at everybody. The only thing not copacetic is attitude, what they teach their young and the Eastern European worker-bees, the not-hiring of whom would be unpopular. You know the word cater. They do that. They're low-key but on to a business model unbeatable.

Sex is the main message, in an old motel like the one your family stayed in driving out to the Grand Canyon. Only better, because here you don't have to hide the shenanigans you got up to one afternoon with the St. Louis teenager one year older than you while everyone was down at the pool. But *here*: two floors of flesh and wifi, a pool with a shaded bar and good food. Try the seared tuna. Come for the conch fritters, stay and slum for the punch. Limitless *chaises longues* (fun thing to say when said properly; Chuck spoke a fluent French). He has thought of investing, but the old owner died and there has been some question about financial restructuring. Key West is getting less and less gay, they say. That more and more the family and middle-class time-share types are moving in to edge out the edgier bohemians who first came here to get way laid-back.

Owen, your Uber is arriving now. There's an Uber in your future. The future's in Uber!

Overall he's not a risk-taker. His main money guy has him down as risk-averse; his main money guy's out in Berkeley straddling the Hayward Fault Line, but warns him about hurricanes and storm surges, reminding him the house is a money-sucking liability that could wipe him out, uninsurable against flood, though for now he's loaded. Rental properties, mutuals, stocks, bonds, figures ticking up regularly, halting at times, dropping then going phoenix again—his portfolio a lottery he can live with. He did not have to—there was always plenty of cash—but in 2008 he'd saved and eaten at home mostly. A freezer full of cabbage soup ready for thaw-out. Not bad for his figure and did wonders for his reflux, especially after he switched from red wine to white.

A tall, naked and tan baldie is reading *In Evil Hour* in the original Spanish, his gray chest hairs rioting above his down-pointing breasts, the nipples jaded by love's heat-seeking tortures.

What Owen loves is that this reader appears not to care, reading steadily, nudely sunning.

When Owen is here at Fantasy House he is one with the presiding spirit of Key West and knows that it is mutable and that one day, capital or crashing wave, it will all be swept away. He loves Fantasy House the way he loves the sleepily indifferent town that hums neon-alive at night.

Daylight in March is heartbreakingly gorgeous and it spreads butter on top of the Conch-cake dominion cooling in the late afternoon. Even the seedy little cigarmakers' houses, of crusty wood half-iced with peeled paint, roof-rust caramel, look good enough to reach out for and taste.

The prettiest kid here is Darius from Bratislava. He wears the Fantasy House t-shirt and a mustache. Nobody rocks a mustache like Darius does. He's not the Marlboro Man but Marlboro Boy. He takes butt breaks out by the ice machine, so what's going through his head? *America—oh, whatever.* His colleague Honza is even sweeter, a hulking, Pilsner-blond hockey player. Not gay, either one of them, but neither gay-unfriendly. Grabbing up damp towels, wiping up ashes.

Their narratives are locally storied: left Eastern Europe on summer visas then dropped off the grid: straightforward. It's the Americans—abject and unnecessarily hungry—luring them in.

"Why aren't you in the pool?"

"Usually only at night."

"Timid! Pussy!"

Owen laughs. Because his heart's spark is Richard, a snowboarder from Breckenridge who is not even thirty and who's trained Olympic finishers before. Knocked out his knee and ankle and had to quit competing. Originally from Provo, Utah. Mormon, yes. Estranged from rich family, check. Currently living in a micro-room around the corner from the outdoor hot tub. Karaoke number of choice on Sundays and Mondays at Bobby's, when local hospitality workers meet for a steam letting-off, "Piano Man." Punches, but doesn't nail each time

. . . if I could get out of this place!

There are so many clichés about the Florida grease catcher trapping the down-circled cast-offs.

Eventually you go someplace else, or you go to AA.

Darius in his hillbilly-tempered Slavic whine says, "Another one?"

"Yes, please."

The Czechs only go so far with the niceties and politesse, like most other Europeans.

They have each other. They come on summer work-study visas and either go through the INS rigmarole legit or disappear below the jungly under-the-table, service-economy grid.

You see Darius and Honza working out in the minute gym behind the locker room after their shifts, giving each other a barbell assist, speaking their private, sinus-serrated Czech.

It's a waiting game. Owen is shooting for only one, though he hopes he's a brief keeper.

He'd like to have a boy in his little house, the one he goes to every night after he makes his rounds. Making breakfast for the boy in the morning, talking to, smelling and tasting him.

It's the only thing missing. He only needs it for so long. Then he'll move on from here.

It is a shell-rock Craftsman from the twenties, mosaic-tile porch, Dade pine defying the chewing of termites inside. It has a nickel-dull, sharply peaked tin roof with a modest cute gable gazing at the languid street scene along the leading edge of the Old Town grading into the New. It is worth a million but was bought for three hundred thousand after the bust that completed the hammering Hurricane Wilma had wrought just previously. He likes to settle in of an evening, think of things past with barely a thought forward. He smells the stain and varnish and the pine-sap trapped just beneath the veneers and dust-patina, and gets further drunk and ready for bed, his body sighing a sigh of useless contentment, because if it didn't sigh he would start crying. It wasn't supposed to end this way but soon this may be the finale, and yet he's not unhappy, is perhaps the tragedy.

He's been to oyster happy hour, half-priced oysters, fifty-cent oysters. Gulf oysters from the Appalachia Bay not as good as the Atlantic ones but okay cocktail-sauced, horseradished and slurped down with icy backwashes of IPA, two dozen. Gregarious, at times controversial Chuck would say, and now Owen knows what he meant, "A decent fresh oyster and particularly a French one should taste like you're licking the nacreous pit of a prepubescent boy. Saline, yanked right from the sea, innocent and surprised." Chuck said much worse things, but the women he walked in San Francisco liked to hoot and approve, applauding. Ready for anything those rich old birds.

Restaurants, their former venue. But no one at oyster happy hour talks to Owen. They're snowbirds from Michigan, retired couples, construction-fed portfolio rats, snowboarding over the dry powder of others' cold, new-fallen calamities under a promisingly clear bluebird sky. That is what Richard calls it, bluebird. Under a poinciana swelling to pod in hopes of blossom. Oh but how, late one night, maybe three in the morning (Fantasy House never closes, not for any holiday, nor nobody), Richard had bitched about his family, his circumstances, even his true fresh beauty.

"I'll come into my grandparents' inheritance with a trust fund when I'm thirty-three. Get it, thirty-three? Jesus supposedly died then? And when that happens fuck everybody else. I hate this place, by the way, I'm just sort of planting myself. I'll tell you more later unless you want to buy me one more Yuengling. I feel like going quiet a while, but you could buy me a Yuengling."

"Sure."

Owen started getting up from the *chaise longue*.

"But nothing's going to happen, right? I just like talking to you. You're cool enough."

"My mother used to call these chase lounges. She didn't know, she said chase lounges."

Each day Richard says he's about to leave, hating it here. But he still hasn't left.

A part of Owen wants him to leave, then the agony of waiting will be over for now, then Owen can start over waiting for something else until he gets tired completely of waiting and can decide to leave, too. He's waiting for others to leave in order to decide for himself to leave. But Richard is special, though it may be axiomatic that every love-object is special until he no longer is, when he shows his true colors, and reminds the potential lover the beloved is nothing special.

One evening, though, Owen left his sweet little house and against his usual habit returned to Fantasy House on his day pass—just to see what would happen, wanting something to happen.

There's no ending to this story, only new opening-ups prefiguring the arrival of the gurney.

He's well-outfitted for the sail, he's beer-and-wine-luffed and he's already pulled out of the harbor. Feels capital, just smooth open flying out, then tacking back to port, all glassy-sweet.

In the meantime, true story: the day after, his best friend in Russian Hill said, "Would you rather Chuck had not come home, instead of his falling and bleeding to death in your arms?"

"Yes."

"You'd prefer it, even though you guys shared that moment, and he smiled up at you?"

"I'd much prefer it," he said, cadging some of Chuck's tony Wesleyan idiom.

The insurance wanted Chuck home, judged him capable of returning home in anticipation of his near-future interment in hospice, and it had been cruel and put Owen in an awkward spot.

Coming home, drug-stupidly, Chuck had said, "I hope I haven't disappointed you."

"But how could you ever disappoint me, darling? I love you."

And he'd meant it, but internally relented. Hating to see Chuck suffer so closely to him.

He's been to the back bar on Duval and had two Yuenglings, though nothing there doing.

But he's so tired. Don't go home, so what else to do? Fantasy House. Get a day pass so you can head back into the horny sinuous deeps of the second floor just off from the rooms. He takes an indoor hot tub; nobody's there, he's sleepy. Take a nap in the dark room where the sex's obscure but sometimes happens under the video monitors playing explicit porn.

He falls asleep alone on a cushioned bench while the silent thankfully volume-down porn plays, and is awakened by a kiss, Richard's kiss.

"Owen, can you fuck me?"

It's so tender. The need for gay sex can be gentle, respectful, affectionate and tender, but he hasn't brought his accoutrement, hasn't brought his cock ring and he hasn't swallowed his blue pill, an organic hard-on enhancer that two hours hence can really work. But they're kissing.

Richard says, "I thought you'd be here."

"You did?"

"I thought you'd be here. I'm so fucked-up."

"Why?"

"My boyfriend Justin and I had a fight."

"I'm sorry."

"I'm so confused and horny. I think he's looking for me. We had an argument and I'm so mad about shit. I don't think I'm mad at him but I'm not sure what I'm mad about."

"Maybe you should talk to him. Maybe you're just tired."

"Maybe. I don't even like you. I mean I think you're cute, but you and me we're nothing and I don't even know what this is about."

"Maybe you should just wait and see if he comes. He knows you're here."

"That's right, but in the meantime."

His hips are narrow and his skin all over is hazelnut silk. Everything Owen never was.

Then Richard lies back on the padded table of the narrow, cramped backroom video space whatever they call it. At each corner of the table is a post and he undoes his towel, raises his legs and curls his feet around two wood posts revealing himself, full-open and spread radiantly, clean.

Owen gets down on his knees still wearing his towel. The young man's anus is a grayish-pink sideways smirk in this light. Tonguing at the aperture, he digs in farther and farther, tasting.

"Now fuck me."

"Sorry babe, I don't think I can."

"Fuck me," Richard repeats on a high poignant note, his thickly lashed eyes closed.

He's beautiful, the young man of almost anyone's desiring, the smooth boy next door.

A boy like this will be gone in a few months. A boy like this always is.

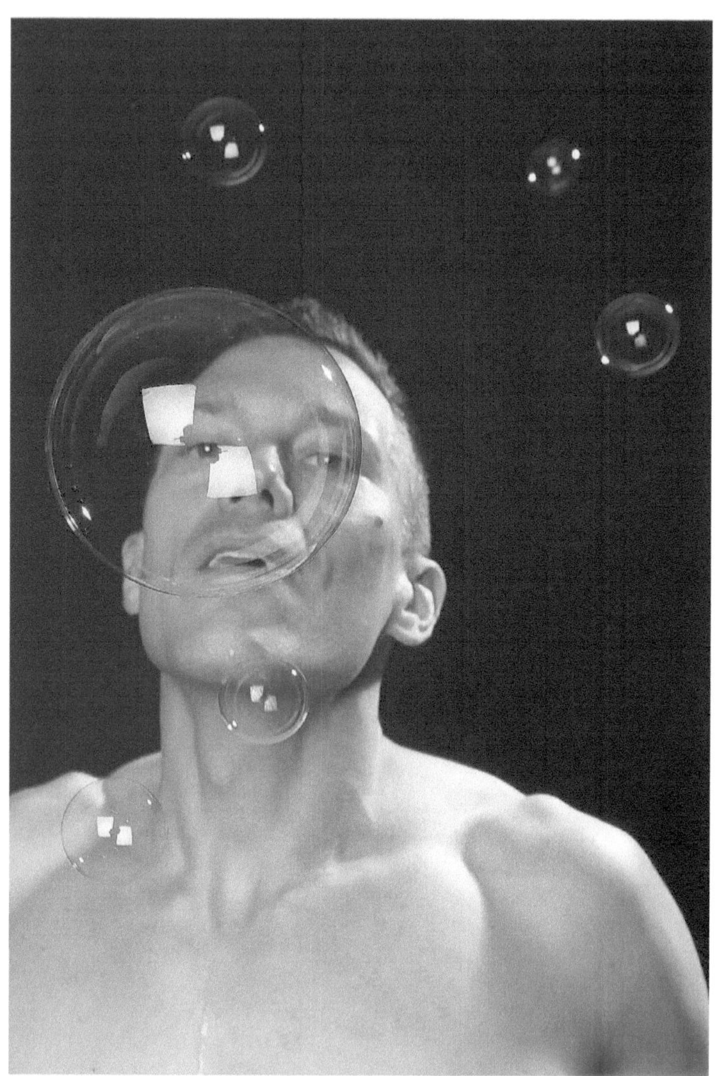

50TH ANNIVERSARY OF A MAN-MADE LAKE

Elizabeth J. Colen and Carol Guess

This morning, dog balked
at a buck in the carport.
I unfasten things
by the side of the road.
6am call. Gray man
and his flatscreen.
Tender with wrinkles,
pre-Stonewall wrists
scarred. I take him
while we watch
the news because this
is how news lets itself
be surprised. Fluff
piece at sunrise. I grip
what I can. The only way
I'm ever touched. Some
combustion in the center
flares, then holds,
collapses.

Some dim lens widens,
contracts. Cat backed
in a shelf, all purr.
Watches the lube bottle, us.
Some sound of slapping,
the TV hums, volume down,
the pictures there flit:
the blonde, the lake, strip
mall, healthy balloons hit
by wind, the blonde

sheen of bubbles
bursting in the bath.
We barely fit, so I
step out, uncork
a towel, cock
the remote. Control
what I can. The buck
stared down leash,
dog, and day. The day
blew morning
coffee cool.
I am, I think, watertight.
Sweat rolls right off. Air-
tight. One sniff, I puff
up again. Cat backed.
A purr. Same slap.
The blonde. Some hint
of boom.

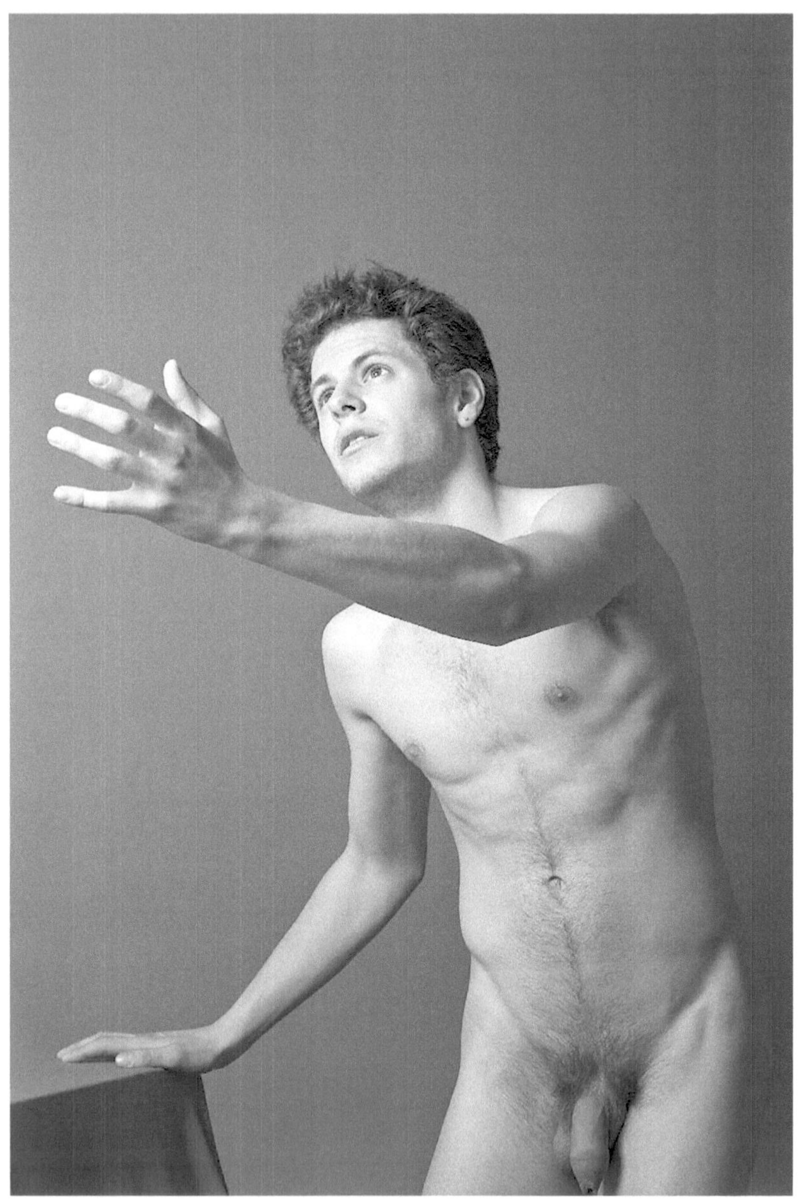

Solo

Richard Michaels

Boom!

Boom!

b-Boom!

Damn!

The musical track is off again. Which means the whole performance is off.

The theatre sound system is an aged CD player with a drive that resists consistency, the CD is equally decrepit, and sometimes the result is ragged. The owner is averse to spending money if he doesn't have to, and very seldom does he feel he has to, so the audio is frequently undependable, spitting forth static or an inadequate volume or, as now, music that skips and stutters, which makes following it an exercise in ad-libbing.

But will anyone notice? Probably not. No one is here to see the New York City Ballet, after all.

But no matter what everyone else thinks, Sal knows that his presentation is wrong. And it is important that the effect be right. Not perfect—he tries for perfection, but nothing is perfect—yet the flow, the appearance, at least, of fluidity has to be maintained. The dance must go on. So he improvises, and he hates doing that because he loses some control of his impact, but he appreciates the challenge, the demands that are forced on him, because he is an artist and his dance is more than routine.

From the moment the bright light illuminates him, he seeks unity, accord, harmony; instead he often must compromise and express only a fragment of his vision, of his expression of his self.

He looks out at the audience. Most of the regulars are here, including the overweight man in the third row who watches Sal each night. As usual, he stares intently and sits with his coat over his lap. Sal doesn't understand the camouflage, since the man's left hand is beneath the coat and the fabric moves up and down. Why doesn't the man just join those who openly stroke their exposed cocks? The theatre won't be raided; it's a private club, with fees and admissions, and unless something drastic happens, the police care not one iota about the men in the audience and the dancers. As a matter of fact, Sal has seen a couple of cops (in civilian clothes, of course) in the ogling spectators, surreptitiously rubbing through their pants their under-cover cocks.

The young man in the fifth row is a newcomer, and he watches as avidly as the overweight man. His eyes are wide, and his mouth forms a circle of surprise and delight. He's handsome in a sort of unfinished way, and Sal's not sure why he's here, why he's not elsewhere attracting the attentions of other nice-looking young lads. Perhaps this is an initiation of some sort.

Halfway back is the man who's asleep, who has consistently slept through Sal's creations. Maybe this is his bedroom. Sal is accustomed to the man's oblivion; still, it would be nice if the man were awake and appreciative. While the dance is of course for the delectation of the spectators, it's not only for them.

So Sal slides a mental shade over the silent sleeper (at least he's not yet snoring) and concentrates on the men who are awake and attentive. The owner (who refers to himself as "the producer") has said that Sal's presentations always draw the greatest crowds, and Sal is pleased that so many men attend his performances so often. He dances only three times a week to avoid overexposure.

He's aware that he's an attractive man, and he's kept himself in good shape, especially for a man approaching middle age. His dancing career is limited, whether he wants to face that fact or not. And he doesn't. But he realizes. He realizes.

So for them all, he dances, for the overweight man, for the faithful, for the newcomer in the fifth row, for the men who have finally ventured into his venue, even for the sleeper, for the cocks unsheathed and concealed, for them all, and for himself.

He works to mask the error in the music, to make it seem that the syncopation is designed and the jagged steps have a system, that everything is choreography, not trial and error. He must also carefully maneuver to avoid the nails in two places on the floor, nails that the owner has promised numerous times to hammer down but has not; and so the dance is dense and dangerous and yet a delight.

Sal slips off his shirt against the *beat, beat, b-beat* of the music, and when the sound stammers into yet another cadence, he transposes his steps into a revised rhythm. Facing away from the watchers, he hangs his shirt on a hook on the back wall of the stage and looks over his shoulder in a way that is intended to be provocative, then slowly strips his strapped undershirt over his head and hangs it also on the hook. Then he turns forward.

He hears a deep inhalation from his observers. He's sure he hears the inhalation. He exercises every day to keep his chest well defined, but tries to avoid appearing muscle-bound. The effort, he is certain, is appreciated by his audience.

Slowly, he begins the lazy, luxurious opening of his jeans, pausing between buttons, sometimes smiling, teasing the watchers. Midway undoing the fly, he stops and takes a few steps to the right as if he were not going to continue offering himself, but he does not stop stretching like a cat. He can feel an electrical spark between his audience and him, and he grins, as if saying to the men, "All right, you've convinced me. I'll give you more," and he runs a hand from one nipple to the other, traces from his neck down to the top of his jeans, into his crotch, releasing another button, another, deliberately disclosing his white briefs.

Already, he is hard.

When the last button is free, he again turns away, and he slides the jeans down his legs, following with his upper body until, as the jeans are at his feet, he is bent over and presenting to his devotees the blinding white of his taut encased ass. He wears no shoes or socks, and he removes the jeans over his feet, then straightens, steps in the broken rhythm of the music to the back wall and hangs his jeans on a hook separate from the shirt and undershirt.

Almost lazily, he faces front again, and he knows that his hardness is outlined by the tight white cotton of his briefs. He strides to the front of the stage the better to reveal himself and stands with his hands on his hips and raises his head and gazes at each individual. The overweight man is fixated on him as the tempo of his hand beneath his coat increases; the novice in the fifth row is running his tongue over his lips, his eyes are, if possible, wider; and the sleeper slumbers on, impervious. As Sal contemplates his audience, he feels the wet spot blossom on the front of his shorts, auguring release and revelation, and he circles the stage, keeping his eyes on his men, as if daring them to scrutinize him, as if daring them to look away.

Center stage, he slides the white briefs down a little, clearing a bit the shrub of hair, stops, and with a look of false modesty, he yet again turns his back to the men and wiggles the shorts over his hips and his legs, once more bending as he does. Now he presents his ass unencumbered, exposed, and he knows that he has a great ass, he has frequently been told so, and he gives it to the watchers unadorned, but only for a short time. Before the exhibition of his ass and its cleft and the glimpse of its darkness become vulgar, he straightens, and with the shorts dangling from a finger over his shoulder glances at the men, waits, waits, then abruptly flings the shorts into the wings of the theatre. He used to throw them into the midst of the spectators, but aside from the expense of constantly replenishing his supply, the tossed underwear often became the focus of attention. Often contests for possession of the moist, marked fabric became quite aggressive, detracting from the next disclosure.

He whirls and faces the men, and this time there is definitely a gasp, because his cock is long and it is thick and it is hard.

He marches to the front of the stage, his cock swinging, and he looks at the men, he looks at his cock, his long thick hard cock, then he looks at the men, grinning, and they all, the men and he, share in the wonder of his cock. And it is a wonder, he can tell from the glittering attention of the overweight man and the young man licking his upper lip and the rest of the men leaning forward, and he can tell from the heft he feels at his groin, the tingle, the increasing urgency, how his cock seems to be a separate creature from him and at the same time an extension reaching far beyond his crotch toward the men, the men, and the music has crescendoed, and he starts the dance anew.

Not for him the bump and grind of a cheap burlesque exhibitionist, but rather an athletic extension of arms and legs and torso and cock, and then he pirouettes and transforms his muscular display into a ballet

> *and he is standing in a meadow with grasses as high as his shoulder, and the waving fingers rustle over his naked body and he rises to meet them and he lifts his head to greet the radiant sun as bright and intense as a spotlight*
>
> *boom*
>
> *far away*
>
> *in front of him is an undulation in the tall luxuriant lawn, and he moves to it, but the undulation is first in*
>
> *one place and then another*
>
> *the grass is whispering to him here—here—come here—there—there—go there*
>
> *and he follows he knows not what to a place he knows not where and yet he knows exactly where he is going and he knows that he must follow and seek*
>
> *the grass whispers*
>
> *and the man stands before him*
>
> *a nude young man*
>
> *handsome in an unfinished sort of way*
>
> *he walks toward the man*
>
> *a sharp pain in his foot*
>
> *he is hard but the young man is not hard*

and it seems terribly important that the young man be hard

so he steps toward the young man

who is now behind him

he turns

b-

the young man regards him with wide eyes and gaping mouth and

what

alarm

in his wide wide eyes

and he too is uneasy

why?

the young man still is not hard

he himself is

he looks from his groin again toward the young man

not there

not anywhere

boom

as he searches for the young man

his stomach churns and his cock is heavy

a sound like snoring tears the air and the now wilted field

and

he stands downstage, as close to the audience as possible. His cock is hard and pulsing and his body is shaking, and the music's *boom-boom-b-booms* arrive at their climax too late after he arrives at his, but the watchers don't care at all about the mistiming and he cares only momentarily because he is coming, he comes without touching himself, spontaneous combustion, he is spurting on the stage and a few of the patrons in the first row, especially the ecstatic man who always sits there hoping for that baptism, and the overweight man in the third row is at a rigid angle to his seat as his hand pumps so fast it's almost a blur, and Sal cannot see the young man, and then he can see nothing as he closes his eyes and abandons himself to his orgasm and waves his body and his hard spurting cock back and forth because he has to let everyone see the fountain of his phallic rainstorm, he can't disappoint anyone. He has something to give to the men, to give to each of them and to all of them, and he is not like the other dancers who appear disinterested in the apex of their act, but he throws back his head and cries out, he howls.

His display is not fraud or illusion or even ostentation; it is authentic; dicks whirl and whiz dizzyingly behind his shuttered lids, and his own cock is the vortex around which the other cocks spin, spouting and spewing into the wet wild air, fountains lightening up the darkness; and pricks pinwheel until he is giddy, the pricks of the men who are rapt at this exultation, his own prick; and there is a fever in him and an intensity and a fury; and he is gripped with a disruptive eruptive ache that can be assuaged only by the consummation bursting forth from his fiery cock; and this is reality, the singular reality, the very existence.

When he's done, when the last drop has been spent, he waits for a moment with his eyes still closed, then opens them and stares at the men with what he intends as a sort of self-effacing satisfaction: the man in the front row wiping his face; the overweight man who seems emotionally and physically drained; but not the young man, his seat is empty—where did he go, why did he go just at the peak of Sal's performance?

Then begins the monetary homage: fives and tens and twenties flutter to the stage. Sal picks up the bills, and he holds them to his still-heaving chest and modestly smiles his gratitude and bows a bit, and then with his head held high in the afterglow of the torrential termination of his dance, Sal strides offstage.

He is followed by applause and whistles and even the stamping of feet. He smiles. He is exhilarated and exhausted, and already he is thinking of the next presentation and wishing that the young man would return.

As usual, without cleaning up, Sal will put on his street costume and leave the theatre, hoping that he doesn't meet any of his admirers, although sometimes he does. He will go to his apartment, which, since the "producer" does not like to spend money, is eclectically and sparsely furnished—only occasionally does he supplement the obeisance his audience pays him—and he will sit on his sofa and think about the performance, and then he will undress and, still without cleaning up, will go to bed and wait for sleep and dreaming.

This is it: the dance.

Tonight's dance is done.

But there will be another dance.

There must always be another dance.

CONTRIBUTORS

'NATHAN BURGOINE's first novel, *Light,* was a finalist for a Lambda Literary Award. He has published dozens of short stories in various anthologies, and his first novella, "In Memorium," is included in *On the Run*. 'Nathan lives in Ottawa with his husband, Daniel, and their husky, Coach. Find him at NathanBurgoine.com.

MICHAEL CARROLL's collection *Little Reef and Other Stories* (Terrace Books, University of Wisconsin Press) won the 2015 Sue Kaufman Prize for First Fiction from the American Academy of Arts and Letters. His stories, reviews and interviews with other authors have appeared online and in a number of print journals and anthologies. He lives in New York.

LOUIS FLINT CECI's poetry has been read on PRI's *Living on Earth*, seen print in *Colorado North Review,* and won an "honorable mention" in *New York* magazine's late lamented literary competition. His short stories have appeared in *Diseased Pariah News*, *Trikone*, and *Jonathan*, and in the anthologies *Queer and Catholic* and *Gay City Vol. 4: At Second Glance*.

ELIZABETH J. COLEN's most recent book is the long poem/lyric essay hybrid, *The Green Condition* (Ricochet Editions, 2014). Forthcoming books include a short story collection, *Your Sick* (Jellyfish Highway, 2016, co-written with Carol Guess and Kelly Magee), and a novel-in-prose-poems, *What Weaponry* (Black Lawrence Press, 2016).

DANIEL ALLEN COX is the author of the novels *Shuck*, *Krakow Melt*, *Basement of Wolves*, *Mouthquake*, and the novella *Tattoo This Madness In*. He co-wrote the screenplay for Bruce LaBruce's 2013 film *Gerontophilia*. Daniel was a

2015 writer-in-residence at the Zvona i Nari Library and Literary Retreat in Ližnjan, Croatia.

LEWIS DESIMONE (www.lewisdesimone.com) is the author of *Chemistry* and *The Heart's History*. His work has appeared in *Jonathan, Chelsea Station, Christopher Street,* and a number of anthologies, including *My Diva: 65 Gay Men on the Women Who Inspire Them*. He's happy to report that in his next novel, nobody dies.

DOT (a.k.a. TOM SCHMIDT) took his name to represent the pixel in a digital photograph and to express his passion for the medium. Dot's books of photographs include *Cured, Sons of God*, and *Guilty Pleasures*. Check out more of Dot's work at www.PhotoByDot.com.

MILES GRIFFIS is a born, raised, and die-hard Colorado boy. You'll find him on steep slopes in the winter skiing, and on switchbacking trails in the summer hiking. His writing focuses on masculinities, queer men, and wilderness. You can find his short stories, screenplays, poems, and essays at milesgriffis.tumblr.com.

CAROL GUESS (www.carolguess.blogspot.com) is the author of fifteen books of poetry and prose, including *Doll Studies: Forensics* and *Tinderbox Lawn.* In 2014 she was awarded the Philolexian Award for Distinguished Literary Achievement by Columbia University. Her most recent book, *With Animal,* was co-written with Kelly Magee. She teaches at Western Washington University.

TREBOR HEALEY (www.treborhealey.com) is the author of three novels, a short story collection, and a book of homoerotic poetry. His forthcoming short story collection, *Eros and Dust*, will be published by Lethe Press in 2016. He has received a Lambda Literary Award, two Publishing Triangle awards, and a Violet Quill award.

MIODRAG KOJADINOVIĆ's literary work has been published in English, Serbian, French, Russian, Portuguese, Chinese (both traditional and simplified), Dutch, Hebrew, German, Hungarian, Frisian, and Slovene, and his photography exhibited or published in North America, Europe, and Asia. Two of his short story collections came out in October 2015 (www.amazon.co.uk//Miodrag-Kojadinovic/e/B015DAZWHM/).

JOHNATHAN LAY is a poet, writer, and former San Francisco go-go boy. He was born in New Orleans and raised in Atlanta, the oldest of eleven children. He received his Master's in Writing from the University of San Francisco, and now resides in his hometown in Georgia, enjoying family, friends, and writing more poetry.

RICHARD WILDE LOPEZ is a New York native and local writer. He has been published online and in print in *Daddy Issues Vol. 1.* He is a scholarship recipient of the Key West Literary Seminar 2015. He enjoys artisanal cheeses, stove top coffee, and reading by the Hudson. His favorite whiskey is Jameson.

RAYMOND LUCZAK (raymondluczak.com) is the author and editor of seventeen books. His latest title is *QDA: A Queer Disability Anthology* (Squares & Rebels). His novel *Men with Their Hands* (Queer Mojo) won first place in the Project: QueerLit Contest 2006. He lives in Minneapolis, Minnesota.

JEFF MANN has published three poetry chapbooks, five full-length books of poetry, two collections of personal essays, a volume of memoir and poetry, three novellas, four novels, and two collections of short fiction. The winner of two Lambda Literary Awards, he teaches creative writing at Virginia Tech.

ALAN MARTINEZ is an architect who writes poems sometimes. "A Piece in the Game" is his second published poem; his first was published in *Christopher Street* in the late 1970's. His high school English teacher insisted that he read Hawthorne's "The Artist of the Beautiful." The italicized lines in his poem are from that story.

VINTON RAFE MCCABE is the author of ten books of nonfiction and one novel, *Death in Venice, California*, which was shortlisted for the Lambda Literary Award for Debut Fiction in 2015. An award-winning poet and playwright and life-long journalist, McCabe also works as a literary critic and reviews for *The New York Journal of Books*.

MIKE MCCLELLAND writes fiction and essays. He spent a decade as an ad man, during which he lived in England, South Africa, and Hong Kong before returning to the U.S.A. He now resides in Georgia with his husband and a menagerie of rescue dogs. Keep up with him at magicmikewrites.com.

STEPHEN MEAD, a resident of New York, is a published artist, writer, maker of short-collage films and sound-collage downloads. If you are at all interested and get the time, search on line for Stephen Mead and the genres of writing or art, or both, and get links to his multi-media work and merchandise.

JIM METZGER (www.edwardbutcher.com) has most recently worked as a math teacher. His writing process evolves, but one seemingly consistent thread seeks to explore the ways in which language activates misunderstanding, manipulation, or empowerment. He has published essays and short fiction, and has had his work performed.

RICHARD MICHAELS appears in the anthologies *Best Gay Erotica Volume 1*, *Best Gay Erotica 2015*, and *Special Forces*. One of his stories is scheduled for the upcoming collection *War-*

lords and Warriors. He has also written for several leading gay magazines.

GREGORY L. NORRIS has written regularly for fiction anthologies, national magazines, and the occasional TV episode and feature film. His career has been profiled numerous times in print, radio, and television interviews. Follow his literary adventures at www.gregorylnorris.blogspot.com.

DAVID PRATT is the author of *Looking After Joey* (Wilde City), the Lambda Award-winning *Bob the Book* (Chelsea Station), and the story collection, *My Movie* (Chelsea Station). He has directed and performed work for the theater in New York City at the Cornelia Street Cafe, Dixon Place, HERE, the Flea, and the New York International Fringe Festival. David lives in Ann Arbor, Michigan.

JIM PROVENZANO (www.jimprovenzano.blogspot.com) is the author of the Lambda Literary Award winner *Every Time I Think of You* and its sequel *Message of Love* (a Lammy Finalist), the novels *PINS, Monkey Suits, Cyclizen*, and the stage adaptation of *PINS*. A journalist in LGBT media for three decades, he lives in San Francisco.

ROB ROSEN (www.therobrosen.com)—author of Sparkle: The Queerest Book You'll Ever Love, Divas Las Vegas, Hot Lava, Southern Fried, Queerwolf, Vamp, Queens of the Apocalypse, Creature Comfort, and Fate, and editor of Lust in Time, Men of the Manor, Best Gay Erotica 2015 and 2016—has had short stories featured in more than two hundred anthologies.

ERIK SCHUCKERS studied writing at Allegheny College and the University of Sheffield. He picked apples, cleaned theaters, and sold books in the U.S. and U.K. before moving into nonprofit work. He lives in Pittsburgh. His poems have appeared in *Assaracus, PANK*, and as part of the *HIV Here & Now Project*, among others.

MARK WARD (astintinyourspolight.wordpress.com) is from Dublin, Ireland. He was the 2015 Poet Laureate for *Glitterwolf* and has been featured in *Assaracus, Storm Cellar, The Good Men Project,* and the anthology *The Myriad Carnival.* He has recently completed a chapbook called *How To Live When Life Subtracts.*

SALOME Wilde (www.salandtalerotica.com) has published dozens of erotic stories featuring characters of diverse orientations in a wide variety of genres, from hard-boiled dicks to the sex lives of inanimate objects. Wilde is also editor of the anthologies *Shakespearotica: Queering the Bard* and *Desire Behind Bars: Lesbian Prison Erotica.*

Acknowledgments

Louis Flint Ceci would like to thank all those who encouraged him to pursue this project, especially Jerry L. Wheeler; fellow authors and editors who gave timely advice on the practical issues of shepherding an anthology from initial call to contributor's contracts to font sizes and proofs, especially Rob Rosen, Raymond Luczak, Ron Suresha, and Brent Hartinger; technical PDF help from Peter Deutch and Matt Cresswell; early readers Remy Ceci and Steve Rushton; and Dot, who responded quickly and gracefully to shifting demands about photo selection, picture size, cropping, and other fiddly details.

Dot would like to thank the models who appear on these pages: Braun, Nic Candito, Colin, Samuel Cuadra, Leon Fox, James, Kyle, Johnathan Lay, Bray Love, Colin Malone, Ali Mushraq, Phillip, Joshua Pritchard, Dev Ray, Gabe Riddle, Joey Russo, Diego Sans, PJ Shields, Cody Evans Silver, and Patrick Stone.

www.ingramcontent.com/pod-product-compliance
Ingram Content Group UK Ltd.
Pitfield, Milton Keynes, MK11 3LW, UK
UKHW041827200726
13854UKWH00002BA/646